The Simple Truth

ABOUT
YOU

DAVID T BASTON

The simple truth about you
© David T Baston 2015

National Library of Australia Cataloguing-in-Publication entry (pbk)

Author: Baston, David T., author.

Title: The simple truth about you / David T Baston.

ISBN: 9780994374561 (paperback)

Subjects: Self-knowledge, Theory of.
                 Self-perception.
                 Awareness--Religious aspects.
                 Spirituality.

Dewey Number: 126

Published by David T Baston and InHouse Publishing
www.inhousepublishing.com.au

IN HOUSE
PUBLISHING

Printed using Envirocare paper

Contents

INTRODUCTION

I spent a moment in Heaven, in the mind of God.

As the limitations of my body were transcended I found my awareness encompassed by a brilliant golden light that emanated the most overwhelming feeling of love and gratitude imaginable. In this moment of awareness beyond time and space, the knowledge of the universe became simply apparent in a dawning moment of understanding as I became one with the light.

This experience is part of a series of what I call 'Revelations of Truth' in which I came to experience myself as simply 'awareness'. The idea of being confined in a body disappeared into the knowledge of the eternal, as my mind expanded to encompass all of creation.

This is not a book on religion, yet it is for all religions. This is not a book on science, yet it holds the answer to creation. This is not a book on psychology, yet it contains the knowledge of the mind.

This is a simple book of logic and reason through which I will attempt to translate my experiences for you, in a practical manner, so that you may demonstrate and experience for yourself the simple truth of what I have come to understand.

Throughout this book is the mention of God, which for many brings about an adverse reaction, usually because of the seemingly dogmatic beliefs held by most monotheistic (one God) religions.

Science would seem to disprove the existence of such a God as the creator of the universe through simple observation, demonstration, and reason.

Through my experiences, I have witnessed the existence of a unified source of life. Call it God or Creation or Life or Divine

Intelligence or Him or Her or whatever you like, but it's just a name and it doesn't really matter. The name is only symbolic of the attributes you assign to it. I choose to use the word God as symbolic for the source of life, but if you don't like this word, then change it to suit yourself.

My experience of God is not the God that most religions believe in. Nor is it this same interpretation of God that science doesn't believe in. It is the God that is the source of all life and as such can be understood from a different perspective that is perhaps yet to be considered by both. I have found that by looking for the commonalities they share, instead of polarising their differences, science and religion can both be reconciled by a singular truth.

As you read on you will find many new concepts that, at face value, may not seem to make much sense. In an effort to understand these concepts it is advised that after each topic you take some time out for reflection and contemplation before you move on. There are also many practical exercises that will give you the opportunity to demonstrate to yourself the validity of these concepts. Try not to skip them and also take some time to contemplate their meaning and together they will begin to make more sense.

I have ordered the concepts and exercises presented in the same step-by-step manner in which I progressed, whilst attempting to reconcile my experiences of being simply 'awareness' with my perception of the physical as it would seem to be. The order is not really important, as everybody would seem to be at their own level of understanding. But whether you are a long-term seeker or just beginning your journey of understanding, I hope the following will serve to help establish or expand upon yours as you progress.

THE AWAKENING

It is over twenty years since I experienced my first 'Revelation of Truth', a life-changing instant of awareness of my true self, my true identity. It was around that time that I was practising a form of meditation in which I would relax myself with conscious breathing and picture in my mind a memory of an event where I felt an intense feeling of love for someone. I would concentrate on this feeling as I inhaled and imagine this feeling as a beautiful golden light filling my body. As I exhaled I would return this feeling back into the universe. As this continued I became more and more at peace, as my body began to fade from my awareness. It was as if I was being drawn out of it and I felt as if a suit of armour was being shed along with all my cares and worries and physical pains and concerns. I was overcome by an overwhelming sense of release and freedom and in that moment came the realisation that my body was insignificant, simply an idea, and nothing to do with my real self at all. As I rose upward and away from the perception of my body I found my awareness surrounded by a soft, white light. I thought about the stories of near death experiences I had heard, where people reported being drawn through a tunnel of white light. And at the end of the tunnel there were usually friends or loved ones there to greet them, but there was no evidence or sense of other beings present.

My attention then shifted to a different perspective. It was as if I was in outer space, still surrounded by this soft, white light, looking down. The Earth was surrounded and consisted of only a bright golden light and there was a beam or tunnel-like form of this light that extended from Earth off into the universe. I looked on in awe of what I was experiencing as thoughts of life on Earth crossed my mind; thoughts of wars and violence and suffering and misery. And as I looked on, I was overcome by an understanding that none of these things were actually happening. I immediately understood that we are all the same, we are all one with each other and the universe, unaware that we are just dreaming of a world where things only seem to happen, which exists only as an illusion, a dream that had no effect on reality as I was experiencing it.

Then my awareness was directed back to the all-encompassing, soft, white light and I felt a deep sense of peace and certainty. I looked into the light, which seemed to go on for infinity; its peace and tranquillity seemed to be drawing me to it. Then I had the thought, "What about my body? Perhaps I should go back?" It was as if a decision had to be reached. Should I stay where I was in peace and freedom or return to my body where I had left it?

An image instantly came to mind of my family and loved ones grieving for me. As I looked upon their sadness it dawned on me again, "It's not real. It's only an illusion. There is no time. And in just an instant we will all be joined together in the awareness of our true selves."

As my attention was once again drawn to the light, I made the decision to stay in this place of peace and freedom. The idea of being confined to a body again was not an option. As I began to move further into the light, I suddenly awakened to the perception of my body again—or so it seemed.

I closed my eyes and tried to go back. The experience was still clear in my mind and I felt an overwhelming yearning to return. But alas, try as I might, I couldn't. I still had an incredible feeling of peace about me and as I looked around to get my bearings the world around me and everything in it seemed to look different. Everything was glowing and radiated a sort of energy or light. It was as if nothing was quite as solid or as certain as it had seemed before. With this new understanding, the understanding that the world is only an idea, a dream, it all seemed to make sense.

The memory of this experience consumed my thoughts for the next couple of weeks, and I would bring the moment to my mind as I meditated. I tried to relive every instant, to gain clarity and understanding, and I still retained a deep feeling of peace and certainty.

The world was now so much brighter and more radiant. Things didn't seem so serious and important anymore and I was happier than I had been for a long time. I felt a sense of destiny in my life. As I drove to work in the mornings, usually at dawn, I experienced a beauty that I had never been aware of before, as the sun rose and the majesty of the day would unfold before me. All was peaceful and still in the magic of the moment.

As the weeks and months passed, this new way of seeing, this heightened awareness, stayed with me. Everything still emitted or rather was encompassed by this soft, white light, which seemed to be everywhere I looked when my mind was still and unoccupied.

THE GARDEN OF EDEN

I recall a beautiful sunny day when I was sitting on a park bench. The park had a small lake and was surrounded by flowering plants and large weeping willows. It was quiet and still. As I brought my awareness to the soft, white light that by now I was used to seeing enveloping the trees and plants, the light became brighter and more encompassing until the whole park and everything in it was just this beautiful, peaceful, white light. The trees and plants were now defined only by this light, as their form became the light itself. Time seemed to stop and the awareness of my body was no more as I too became a part of the light, so radiant and peaceful.

I think of this experience as symbolic of the idea of the Garden of Eden, a place of innocence, of untouched beauty, serene and complete in itself, timeless and unopposed.

I'm not sure how long this experience lasted. I remember the awareness of my body returning and the intensity of the light subsiding and the appearance of form returning. Then there I was as before, sitting on the park bench, peacefully aware of the light that encompassed the trees.

As the months and the years passed, the attraction of the world would see this new awareness slowly become dormant.

I was busy with work and commitments, plans and worldly goals, and I forgot to just be still and look at the beauty around me. The light seemed to disappear from my awareness, as my dreams of the world took hold again.

OUT-OF-BODY AWARENESS

It would be some years before the next experience would take place. I remember driving up the coast to a beach some several hours away from home. When I came to my destination I decided to park on the cliffs overlooking the coastline. The sun was just rising over the ocean with its golden light beginning to envelop the darkness. Inland it was still dark and there was a full moon still high in the sky and the clouds became purple in colour as the sun continued to rise. It was still and peaceful and I began to recall how I used to experience the light; this all-encompassing light that the rising sun reminded me of. I looked on at the ocean, watching the waves ebb and flow and in the next moment I, once again, became unaware of my body. My awareness seemed to enlarge to encompass the whole world. It was as if the world existed only as an idea, a vision in my mind. And from within this awareness I experienced the idea of the ebb and flow of all the oceans of the world as an onlooker, outside of time and place. It was truly an awe-inspiring experience of freedom and understanding.

I recall another similar experience. It was on the eve of the millennium and I was on the foreshore of the harbour celebrating this milestone in humanity with tens of thousands of others. As the countdown began, I started thinking about the idea that everybody on the planet was united in this moment of celebration. If nothing else in the world could, we would all share this moment together as one. I looked on at the endless crowds of people as I started to feel a sense of oneness with them. As the fireworks began to erupt, my awareness seemed to enlarge to encompass the whole world and, as an onlooker, I experienced myself as being connected to everyone on the planet. This connectedness was in the knowledge that we are all a part of the oneness of creation, total and complete, nobody left outside, united in eternity, united with each other, united in God. Then as the perception of my body returned, I continued to watch the fireworks with a deep sense of unity, peace, and surety.

As the years passed I had many moments of deep insight or understanding and always in the background I could feel a sort of guiding force looking out for me, and there was a sense that I was not alone in the world. My intuition became more apparent and compelling and as I followed its guidance it always resulted in some form of benefit to my perceived circumstances. I even averted several car accidents as a result. There was also a feeling that I still had a purpose to fulfil, an unfolding of some sort of grand plan that I was yet to become aware of and that would present itself to me when the conditions were right.

SEEKING

As somebody that always questioned everything and was never satisfied with easy answers, I would come to challenge every belief that I had ever held about the world and everything in it. For even though my first out-of-body experience is just a memory now, I had a yearning to fully understand it in relation to myself. What I had experienced was more real to me than anything I had ever experienced in the world and the truth of its revelation was undeniable. It started to become clear that somehow there was a way to reconcile this truth so that my awareness and the truth became one.

Science was my passion and even as a young child my curiosity was never satisfied with easy answers. I believed that the mysteries of the universe could be better explained by the discoveries of science as my thirst for understanding grew. So in my usual questioning fashion, I began to seek the way to understand myself, to answer the big question of 'Who am I?' I looked for the answer in science, in the hope that there could be some piece of the puzzle to find there.

I spent time researching quantum physics, to gain perspective through the understanding of the atom and subatomic particles; the building blocks of life, as they are thought of by physicists and quantum engineers. There are many experimental observations put forward to qualify their theories but the common thread of agreement is that they really can't explain the reality of form or creation (as they suggest it is).

Over the years I found many commonalities in various other scientific observations and findings, all of which would seem to point to a singular truth, but the more questions that were answered, the more they would seem to pose.

As a child I went to church regularly and in my early teens attended a Christian school for some time. I both heard and read the story of Genesis and the bible's explanation of creation, but it just seemed to be too unbelievable to accept as the truth. For example, who wrote the book of Genesis? If there was only God in the beginning, who created Heaven and Earth, then who was there at the time to witness it and be able to write about it? Moses, who was born thousands of years after the fact? I remember always asking questions of the pastor in hope of gaining more understanding about creation but I must have worn thin his patience as most of my questions were dismissed or left unanswered. I believed in God but not in the God that they were selling, an unloving God that cast us out of Heaven, a fearful God that would judge us all and punish us for our sins with everlasting damnation to hell. I found it hard to accept the idea that to 'fear God' is the way to live our lives in the hope that we were good enough to gain entry to Heaven. This was not the God I wanted to believe in. It just didn't make sense. The God I believed in was surely only about love.

Now as an adult and in the nature of the seekers of truth I thought that I would give religion another go. Perhaps now I would be able to better understand and interpret the scriptures and perhaps even rationalise the teachings in relation to my experiences. As I began to read I came across a quote from the bible that stated something like 'to know thyself is to know God'.

It just seemed to dawn on me again that this was all I needed to know, the only answer I needed to find. There was no need to look anywhere else. After all, how hard could it be to realise myself, since wherever I went, there I was. This quote would now become the only basis for my seeking. I had already experienced myself as beyond the body and now the realisation that this was the answer to all my questions became apparent: just to simply 'know myself'.

Around this time I began to study other religions to see if I could discover more about myself from different religious perspectives. I would seek only for the similarities in the beliefs that I studied, with the idea that there must be a singular truth to be found. I studied Buddhism, Hinduism, and various other eastern and western philosophies, including the more obscure, ancient tribal beliefs such as the Aboriginal Dreamtime. I gained great insight into the meaning of their ideology and beliefs but the common thread that stuck out for me was the idea that 'we are all one' and 'to know the true nature of yourself is to know God'.

NEW AGE BELIEFS

With the internet being the largest source of information available, the ideas and beliefs of the world were all there to explore. I spent countless hours sifting through everything from spirit guides to psychic abilities, from light healing to mind powers, from witchcraft to extra-terrestrial intervention theories. I also read many books on spiritualism, afterlife experiences and accounts, the power of the mind, the law of attraction, etc. Once again I would look only for the similarities in the content as more pieces of the puzzle seemed to fit my out-of-body experiences.

TRUTH IN THE AFTERLIFE

When I was younger I used to wonder about the afterlife. For example, is there some aspect of myself that continues beyond the physical? And if so, is there really such a place where this aspect will go after physical death? Is there a heaven and a hell? Will I see God and know the truth of myself? Or will I just cease to exist?

It would seem that I would have to die to find out. But how can it be that the answer to life could only be found in death? It just didn't make sense. Surely life holds the answer to life? So what can there be to know about life through death if death is life's end? If life continues beyond the physical in some other form, then surely this aspect of myself exists during this life and can be known now. If death is only the end of the body and my true self or spirit is beyond the body then physical life can have no bearing or influence on my spirit, being always and forever what I really am. The idea of death is simply a mistake in understanding; it is the acceptance of the belief that you are different and separate from the source of life itself.

As a teenager I believed in the idea of lingering spirits as I once experienced what seemed to be a ghost/spirit, at around the age of sixteen.

As I recall, it was early one evening. I was with a friend of mine, Steve, and his girlfriend. We went to Steve's father's house to check on it while he was away. It was an old fibro house that was divided down the middle with a wall that separated the house in two. Steve's father lived on one side and the other half was occupied by a friend of his who had recently died in the house. After we checked the interior of the house we all got back in the car. I was in the backseat, and my friend and his girlfriend were in the front. As we were about to leave Steve noticed that he'd forgotten to move the goat that was tied up and had depleted its food supply. He got out of the car and went to tend to the goat.

The car was parked in the driveway, alongside the part of the house that the man had died in. I casually looked back at the house and in the window noticed the figure of a man, just standing there, looking back at me. The hairs on my neck stood up, as fear surged through my body. I looked away for a couple of seconds then looked back. The figure was still there, looking at me. This time my fear was replaced with a sense of peace. The figure in the window was of a small, stocky, balding man with hair only on the sides of his head and as I looked at him I noticed that he appeared to be somewhat transparent and that his features were shadow-like in appearance.

I won't suggest that I communicated with him but I just seemed to sense that he was looking on in bewilderment as if he was saying, "Who are you? What are you doing here?" We looked at each other for what seemed to be about five or six seconds, then I turned in excitement to the girl in the front seat, telling her to look at the window. But when we turned to look, the figure had disappeared.

When Steve returned, I explained what I had seen and described the ghost's appearance. Steve said in disbelief, "That's the exact description of Dad's friend who died in the house." We checked the doors and windows again but all were locked and as there didn't seem to be any evidence of forced entry, we left.

I personally know several people who believe they can see spirits and some suggest that they can even communicate with them. I have often talked with them about their encounters and asked the questions, "What is it like on the other side? What about God?" in the hope of some sort of guidance or message from the afterlife. But usually the answers were vague at best and in some instances I was told that the spirits were not supposed to divulge the truth.

I joined a spiritualist group as I continued my seeking. The classes were concerned with helping people to develop their psychic abilities such as clairvoyance and spiritual communication. There were about twelve of us, mainly women, attending the weekly classes, most of whom believed they had some sort of psychic ability. The couple who ran the classes believed they could communicate with the afterlife. The woman was said to be a medium, meaning spirits could communicate through her physical form. At times, she would seem to take on different voices and personalities and she stated that she often facilitated the moving on of spirits that were still earth-bound. Her husband was into spiritual energies and cleansing rituals, using crystals, drums, incense, and other charms.

I approached the classes with an open mind, sure that I would discover something about myself that was yet to be revealed.

One of the first topics to be discussed was the idea that the body consists of energy of both a positive and a negative nature and that our bodies are encompassed by an energy field called the aura and contain seven internal energy fields called chakras. It was suggested that our physical and spiritual wellbeing is in direct relationship to how these energy fields are balanced and through exercises like meditation we can bring these energies into alignment and realise our true nature. Also covered in this topic was the idea that you could, and in fact needed to, protect yourself from negative energies that could attach themselves to you from other people or from an environment of social disharmony, such as a community carpark. Once attached, these energies would then manifest themselves in your life in the guises of emotional distress, anger, depression, or even physical sickness. It was believed that a daily protection ritual was needed in order to repel these negative forces and to keep you safe and well.

I could relate to the aura bit, as I could see that for myself, but as for the idea of protecting myself from negative energies that were lurking about ready to attach themselves to me—well, I couldn't see the truth in that idea, for I already understood that negative feelings and emotions were the direct result of thinking negative thoughts. I understood that I was responsible for my thinking and emotional wellbeing and if I felt depressed it had nothing to do with anything outside of my present thoughts. It used to feel natural for me to look for somewhere to lay the blame for how I felt, but once I realised there was no one to blame but my own thoughts then life became more peaceful and I was in control.

As the weeks went on I attended the classes that were usually centred around some sort of guided meditation in which I often found my mind wandering off on some other tangent. "I am here to get answers. I can meditate at home," I thought. But I felt sure I was there for a reason and I would continue to attend until it was realised.

There weren't many opportunities to get one of the teachers alone to ask the questions I wanted the answers to, as there was always competition for their time from the other students. So I seized every opportunity I could.

I recall, in one of the earlier classes, we were discussing various ideas from books we had read and one of the teachers stated that they hadn't read spiritual books for over twenty years, as all of their learning was directed by spirit. "Great," I thought, "this guy will have all the answers." I asked him about the white light that I could see around everything and he suggested that, being white, it was of a very spiritual nature. I asked him what it meant and why I could see it, but he just seemed to go blank and didn't respond.

Then the conversation turned to spirit guides and I asked him, "If we all have a spirit guide who is of a higher spiritual understanding than we are, why is it they don't impart this knowledge to those who can communicate with them? How is it that the secrets of the afterlife are not directly communicated so that we can all understand them?" His response was that the spirits were not supposed to reveal the secrets and that we would have to learn our own lessons, with their guidance of course. Well, obviously my next question was, "Who is it that says they are not supposed to tell?" to which there was no reply.

Come on, I thought, *you must have all the answers, being taught by spirits for the last twenty years!* Well maybe he did and maybe he didn't; either way he wasn't letting on. *So what am I here to learn?* I thought.

From what I had observed in the classes it seemed that the underlying beliefs of the teachers were that we are essentially spirits having a physical experience in the world. The world, being just one plane of many realities, existing as a form of physical energy in which individual spirits inhabit bodies from birth to death for the purpose of learning specific things to add to the progression of their spiritual selves.

Through my experiences/revelations it was simply understood that in the oneness of creation there are no separate beings or spirits that inhabit separate bodies. If this was the information they were receiving from spirits then it would seem that, even in the so-called afterlife, the answers to the big questions were still not fully realised and that it was merely another form of the same dream of separation called by another name. After death you will simply realise that you never were just a body, yet will still continue dreaming the dream of separation.

Then I thought about an exercise where we used a crystal pendulum to determine yes/no answers to specific questions. We were told, "It only works if you believe it will." And that was my dawning moment, the reason why I was there. To reinforce my understanding that everything is only what I believed it to be, just an idea, an illusion, a dream that we are all dreaming.

So, wasting no more time, I moved on. I still had many more questions I needed to find the answers to and somewhere they were waiting for me.

THE LIGHT

I often questioned myself about the light I could see around just about everything I observed when my mind was still. It was a soft, white light that seemed to encompass everything that I looked at. I started to meditate with my eyes open as I found it easier to still my thoughts, and the more attention I gave the light, the brighter it became and the more peaceful I felt. Sometimes the light became more intense, as the form of the objects seemed to become merely a shadow before it, and sometimes the light streaked skyward, up and away from the object, always on a background of peace and serenity. Even at night, when I sat in my yard looking at the trees, the light was shining in the darkness, lighting the sky.

I remember one afternoon I was in my yard meditating, open-eyed, focussing my attention on the light and thinking of its source, when in an instant the world just disappeared from my sight. It was as if I travelled at light speed out and away from the perception of my body. As my awareness seemed to enlarge I was overcome with a deep sense of knowing that the world was simply not real and that everything I had ever believed about it was just an illusion. The truth of myself was beyond the idea of the world. In the next moment my perception returned as everything seemed to reappear before my eyes, with its seeming reality less believable.

As my intention to see the light became more frequent, I experienced many more 'light moments', as I call them. I found the light easier to see when I just allowed it to be rather than trying to make some sort of effort to see it. In an effort to understand it, I came across many ideas that suggested it was a form of energy or radiation that everything emits. But I knew there was more to it than just that, as I had experienced myself as being one with this light before.

I often saw the light around people, the soft, white light that at times would appear as if it were following them. I'd describe it as a shadow of light that moved with their every movement and seemed to be the background to their form. Sometimes it would suddenly catch my attention as people crossed my line of vision and at times would seem more real than the body it encompassed.

Then one afternoon I was sitting in my yard watching the light that surrounded the trees and my young daughter and her friend were swimming in the pool in front of me. As I looked at them, with the intention of seeing the light around them, they began to shine in the most beautiful, golden light. It was all around them and even seemed to radiate through their form. It was as if they became the light itself, similar to what I'd experienced in the park some time before, as described in the section 'The Garden of Eden'. However, this time the light was brilliant and golden. The feeling I got from this light was a deep sense of overwhelming love, innocence, and appreciation all rolled into one, arising from a background of peace and stillness. I had experienced this golden light before in my experience of God and understood this light to be the truth of ourselves.

Soon afterwards I started to see the colours of my body's own aura. The first time it happened, I was observing the soft, white light that I was used to seeing, surrounding my hands, when suddenly it became a vivid blue-green colour. As I looked on, I could see that the light was streaking from my fingertips for some two or three inches.

I had seen the same thing in a video about the body's life force. It was the same blue light that they had captured on film using some sort of special lens or photographic technique.

As I started to see colour more frequently, I began to experience what is referred to as 'colour aura'. This is the idea that different colours radiate a specific colour aura. For example: when I worked in construction, everybody wore high visibility fluorescent yellow clothing. As a result, everywhere I looked I would see a vibrant purple light that seemed to surround everyone. Sometimes, whilst driving, I'd see a red haze around the green traffic signs as I approached them, and colour surrounding the other cars on the road.

At times, usually in the evening, I sat in my yard with my attention focused on the light shining from the trees and became conscious of what seemed to be a sort of energy radiating from my body. It seemed to pulsate from my being, swirling around me like smoke in the wind.

FROM THE PERSPECTIVE OF AWARENESS

Once I took a trip to the beach in a local national park. The beach was set in a cove and was surrounded by small cliffs on either side. There was a short ten-minute walk through the bush to a cliff overlooking the beach and out across the ocean. I thought it would be a good spot to meditate as it was quiet and also very beautiful.

I sat on a bench looking out to sea, the small waves were crashing on the rocks below, and my mind was peaceful and still. I began thinking about the idea of eternity and the oneness of creation and I started to meditate, open-eyed, with the idea that I was one with the waves that were rolling in and that, in a timeless state, the waves were a part of my very being, eternal. Then once again, the perception of my body was no more. My awareness seemed to enlarge to encompass everything around me. It was if I became awareness itself and the beach, the cliffs, the ocean, and everything around me became part of this awareness, complete and whole. With this awareness came a deep sense of unity and an understanding that seemed to deny the very existence of my body.

THROUGH THE EYES OF AWARENESS

One late afternoon I went to visit some friends of mine who lived about half-an-hour from my home. When I arrived they were both in their front yard, doing some gardening. It was a beautiful garden with well-kept lawns and flowering trees and plants. I parked on the street and walked across the road to greet them. As they finished up their tasks and I stood there looking on at the garden, the sun was setting over the mountains. The sky was orange and red as the sun shone from behind the clouds and the street was still and peaceful.

I became aware of the light that I was now used to seeing encompassing everything around me. My thoughts became still, as I took in the beauty and majesty of the moment. In an instant, my awareness shifted from my body to the perspective of an onlooker, an observer of myself. It was as if I was seeing from beyond the confines of my body, from a position in space that seemed to be in the background of myself.

As my friends came into my line of vision, it was as if I was looking on them through a sort of tunnel of light from beyond the world, from a different dimension. The image of them seemed to be like a projection from within my awareness. Their form consisted only of light and there was a sense of overwhelming peace and love for them in the background.

As the moment subsided and my awareness returned to the perspective of the body, this wonderful feeling of peace and love lingered in my mind for quite some time after.

I had another experience quite similar to this one as I was walking down my street one day. As I walked, the awareness of the light radiating from everything around me was my only focus, as my mind became still and my thoughts became singular. Once again, my awareness seemed to shift position from my body's perception to that of an observer looking out from an alternate state of awareness. An awareness that seemed to encompass my very being. The street before me and all it contained was like a projection. It was as if I was watching a film clip from behind the projection, where all was light and what I was experiencing was understood to be reality beyond perception.

Soon after this experience I started to see what can only be described as static or particles of energy, similar to a film projection or a TV screen with no broadcast that seemed to fill the space between everything around me. It was like being in a light rain and the forms around me would appear to be not quite solid, as if they too consisted only of this rain-like static.

As this static became more and more apparent I decided to have my eyes checked to see if they were deteriorating, but the diagnosis was that my eyes were healthy and my vision was normal.

THE WAY FORWARD

The world didn't seem to be quite so real anymore, as my thoughts turned more consistently towards the light. I would more frequently experience dawning moments of understanding where the unreality of the world would become apparent and the foundations of my beliefs were recognised as resting on illusion. It was as if I was in some sort of transitional stage where I didn't quite exist in the world, yet was still bound by the constraints of my perception of it. The thoughts of my experiences were becoming all-consuming, as my desire to become a part of them dominated my every conscious thought and action.

I was meditating daily, sometimes for hours at a time, in an attempt to make permanent this wonderful feeling of peace and unity. This was all I desired as it seemed to me to be more real than anything I had ever experienced in the world.

I was simply bursting to share what I was experiencing and had come to understand with somebody, anybody. I had never told anyone about what I was experiencing and I just couldn't hold it in any longer. I felt like everyone should know but I didn't know anyone who I thought would understand. I would have liked somebody in a position of influence, like a pastor or priest, to listen and perhaps accept what I had to tell them and maybe even allow me to share my experiences with their followers. But from my experience with religions it seemed unlikely, as they all had their own interpretations of the truth and what they believed in was usually never questioned.

Reflecting on my own research and study of various religions and beliefs, I found there was an underlying truth that they shared. *Wouldn't it be great if there was a faith that encompassed this truth by focusing on the similarities they share, instead of polarising their differences?* I thought. I had never heard of such a faith but it seemed like a great idea, like something that could and should exist if there was any hope for peace in the world. "Maybe there is such a belief, somewhere," I thought, "and if there is, maybe they will want to listen."

But where do I look?

The answer soon became apparent through what seemed to be a chain of unrelated circumstances. Around this time I was off work, awaiting an operation on my arm. As part of my treatment I went to the local physiotherapist twice a week for several months. She mentioned that she belonged to the Anglican Church, which she regularly attended with her children and invited me to a seminar at her children's Christian college. There was to be a guest speaker talking about science and religion and she thought that perhaps I would find it interesting. *Yes I would,* I thought, and accepted her invitation.

When I arrived the place was packed. There was an entire hall filled with people sitting, facing the guest speakers' pulpit. Another adjacent hall of similar size was filled with people facing a large projection screen and the foyer was also filled with people sitting on the floor facing several TV screens that were broadcasting the seminar. *This guy must be good,* I thought, *attracting all these people, eagerly awaiting what he has to say.* I took my place on the floor of the foyer, under some stairs with a TV screen just visible amongst the people.

As the speaker commenced it soon became apparent that the purpose of the seminar was to refute statements made by the well-known atheist, Richard Dawkins, about scientific evidence that undermined the relevance of certain bible scriptures relating to creation. It seemed more of the polarisation of differences that I had experienced before; not quite what I had expected.

It didn't hold my attention very long as I suddenly became conscious of the ghost-like shadows of light that surrounded all of the people in my immediate vicinity. I sat there for about half-an-hour, quietly taking in this lovely sight. *So it wasn't a waste of time after all*, I thought. The presence of the light was beautifully peaceful and I felt a sort of unity with these strangers, gathered here for the same reason, to hear the truth, to gain some sort of new understanding and to find the answers we all sought.

My next visit to the physiotherapist would give me the answer I was looking for. Our conversation turned to the seminar and she asked what I thought about it. I told her that it wasn't quite what I'd expected and that I didn't learn anything new. It seemed to be just an argument based on differences. I said, "Wouldn't it be good if there was a place that accepted all religions and beliefs?" to which she answered, "Oh, that's the Baha'i faith, isn't it?"

I hadn't come across this faith in my religious seeking but she seemed sure that this was the place where all religions were accepted as equal. I couldn't wait to get home to google it and find out more.

On the Baha'i website, I discovered that the acceptance of other religions was one of their core values. I came across a transcript written in poetic form, by their accepted prophet Baha'u'llah, called *The Seven Valleys*. It is about the journey of the spirit through seven states of awareness that ultimately results in the awakening of yourself to God. As I read on, it was as if it was speaking to me about the journey I found myself on. The words seemed to be affirming themselves in my mind as I recognised the truth in what I was reading and had come to understand through my experiences. Finally I found the answer, shown to me by my physiotherapist—the last place I would have thought to look.

The next day I made up my mind to visit the Baha'i temple, which was some hours away. I felt sure that there would be somebody there who'd listen to me and even perhaps understand what I was experiencing.

The trip was filled with excitement and anticipation and before I knew it the temple was in sight. It was set in beautiful flowering gardens and had a structure similar in design to that of a middle-eastern mosque with a tall dome at its centre. At the temple entrance there was a petite, older woman there to greet me. As I looked on her, she seemed almost transparent, shimmering in the beautiful golden light that I had seen before. She smiled at me and handed me some information and I felt a sense of peace and reassurance that I had come to the right place. I sat in stillness, taking in the majesty of the building for several minutes and then made my way to the information centre to find somebody to talk to.

The information centre was set up in order to show the progression of the faith, starting with visuals and information about the history of the faith through to a brief video presentation of its modern-day structure and implementation.

A woman approached me and introduced herself as Martha. She asked if I would like any information regarding the faith. As I began to respond, I became overwhelmed with the emotions I had been carrying around with me; the sense of compounding frustration, the need for release, and the need to share my experiences with someone who would understand what was happening to me. I simply broke down in tears with the relief of finally being able to share what I had been experiencing.

She directed me to a more private area of the centre and I began to tell her of my experiences while she sat and listened. She seemed to be a bit bewildered by some of the things that I was saying but she didn't ask any questions. She just sat there and let me vent all of my frustration, as I sobbed between sentences.

When I had finished talking and began to regain my composure, she quietly got up and retrieved a small book from a shelf titled *The Hidden Words*. She presented the book to me and said with a smile, "This is my gift to you." I responded with gratitude to her kindness and said, "You've given me so much more than that, more than you'll ever know."

She seemed to be humbled by what I said, but the feeling of relief I felt for being able to talk to someone about my experiences was indescribable. Martha took my contact details and said that she would forward them to a group closer to my home, so that I might be able to more fully explore the faith. We shared a hug as we parted. *Finally,* I thought, *I have found somewhere to go to share my experiences, with others who share my ideas of unity and will perhaps be open to what I have to say.*

Several weeks passed before I received a phone call from a man with a Middle Eastern accent inviting me to attend a weekly Baha'i meeting that he held at his home. I gladly accepted his invitation, with the relief that someone had at last called. During the weeks that I waited for contact, I continued to read a book I had come across some time earlier called *A Course in Miracles* by Helen Schucman, the title of which seemed to be appearing everywhere I turned, as if I was being guided to it.

For those who are unfamiliar with *A Course in Miracles*, the book is in two main sections; there are thirty-two chapters of text in one section and the other part is a course that consists of one lesson per day for 365 days. The lessons are easy and are presented as simply an idea to think about during your day.

In short, *A Course in Miracles* is about knowing your true self, an idea that I had already embraced as the goal of my seeking. The text seemed very familiar to me, as if my out-of-body experiences were being explained in a way that made complete sense, as they had whilst reading *The Seven Valleys*. Both texts seemed to promote a shift in understanding, a different way to think about things that I'd never considered before.

I had always been the questioning type, never satisfied with easy answers even as a child, but through the course I would come to question everything that I had ever believed to be true about myself and even the very fabric of my perceived reality. The more I questioned, the more I would come to understand and the more the illusion of myself would become apparent. Finally my out-of-body experiences and the truth of their meaning were becoming one.

TRANSFORMATION

This open way of questioning everything now became my way of life and the truth of myself was becoming more apparent as the grasp on my firmly held beliefs were loosening, to be replaced with the light of understanding. All of my anger, all of my cares, and all of my worries simply disappeared before me into the nothingness from whence they came. They were replaced with an almost constant feeling of peace and certainty.

The Baha'i faith was very different from other religions I had been involved with. The ideas and teachings contained in the writings seemed to be very modern, yet echoed the eastern philosophies of ancient times. They encouraged the seeking out of truth through exploring avenues such as science and other religions by bringing to question your own beliefs. There was no pastor or priest to interpret the meaning of the verses for you, as it was up to the individual to interpret their meaning through personal understanding and group sharing.

The faith is directed towards the love and unity of mankind and the building of a new world where peace and harmony abide, accepting all as equals in God's plan. This idea resonated in my mind, as I eagerly read the writings and attended the weekly group meeting, from which I always returned home with a new idea or concept to explore. It seemed like finally all the pieces were starting to come together.

As I continued to explore the writings of the Baha'i faith I would often experience dawning moments of recognition or association as both the course in miracles and the Baha'i writings were pointing towards a singular truth that seemed to bear witness to the revelations I had experienced during my out-of-body moments. The way before me was becoming clear. The last useless journey away from myself was now over and with clear direction this transitional period of being neither here nor there seemed to magnify, as I left the old ideas of reality behind and embraced the new.

I attended the weekly Baha'i meetings for about eighteen months, the host of which had been involved in the faith for over forty years and had a wealth of knowledge about the faith and its writings. Our discussions would often last for hours, as we shared our understanding and interpretations of the writings always with acceptance for what the other had to say, even if we didn't always agree.

After the passing of Baha'u'llah, some 180 years ago, the responsibility for the faith was passed down to his son and then to his grandson and then to the assigned custodians of the faith. I found their writings to be somewhat departed from, and in some cases a misinterpretation of, the wisdom of Baha'u'llah as I understood it. The focus of their writings seemed to be more about the physical aspects of life, with the idea that the only true purpose of life is to prepare for death. Also alluded to were the ideas of 'sacrifice in the name of God' and 'punishment as justice' and living in the 'fear of God'—so far removed from the original writings of Baha'u'llah that speak of peace and love and unity. I seemed to come to a sort of impasse. Whereas my experiences/ revelations were confirmed by the wisdom of Baha'u'llah, the writings of his successors seemed to be contradictory and coming from a lack of understanding. So, with the words of Baha'u'llah firmly imprinted in my heart and mind, I continued on the journey to the awareness of myself.

THE UNIVERSE WITHIN

I have a friend who, like me, shares an interest in science and philosophy and the desire to understand creation. One day we were discussing various quantum theories and one of the topics discussed was the idea that the entire universe is essentially made up of atoms or particles of energy that consist of predominantly empty space. According to an article in the science journal 'Scientific American', the human body is like a universe unto itself, consisting of as many atoms as the known universe has stars; billions upon billions.

In my own tangent of thought, I likened the body to the atoms that make up the entire universe, and reasoned that it is exactly the same in every respect. Sub-atomic particles, for example protons, neutrons, and electrons, are identical in all forms throughout the universe and it is only the way these particles come together or are grouped that seem to establish the differences in form. I concluded that, from the perspective of form, my body and the universe are identical in nature, as the essence of my body and the entire universe are one and the same.

This idea resonated in my mind, as if I had had a dawning moment of insight. Later that day, whilst still pondering this idea, the world once again vanished from my perception and it was as if only my awareness remained. It seemed as if I was in outer space, formless, at one with the entire universe. And then a vision of my first out-of-body moment flashed in my mind, reminding me of the experience I'd had over twenty years ago and reinforcing the understanding that '**I am** one with the universe and the world is nothing more than an idea, an illusion, where nothing real ever happens or ever will'. It was the same joining with the knowledge of the eternal that I had experienced several times before and in the next moment I found myself back in the perception of my body.

I have no control over these experiences. They seem to happen at random, sometimes during my open-eyed meditation practice and sometimes even in the midst of activity. Some occur within weeks of each other and sometimes they are months apart. It seems that they always occur when I have a particular question in mind, with the answers or revelations always pointing to the same understanding.

OUR CREATION

I was driving home one day thinking about creation. Creation of the world, creation of the universe, my creation. I pondered the idea of the big bang theory, the moment when everything is thought to have begun, trying to imagine what it was like. I wondered about the possibility that I had begun this way, as a result of evolution, of something that just seemed to come about over millions of years.

How was I created?

I asked the question and then the answer came.

It was as if I was instantaneously encompassed by the most beautiful golden light. All awareness of my body, my surroundings, and even the fact that I was driving was non-existent. Time stopped and as I was encompassed by this light it became all there was and I became a part of the light that seemed to emanate from a presence of which there was a feeling of overwhelming peace and love, like the love for a child, innocent and pure. My appreciation of this love made the feeling more intense and I seemed to sense a warm, welcoming smile, which flowed from the source of this love to my awareness. In a moment of recognition or knowing, it just seemed all so obvious that this was God, the source of my creation, the truth of my identity. This was spirit itself, being the ever expanding love that I share with all creation, timeless, beyond perception, beyond description.

Then, just as suddenly, I awoke to the seeming reality of driving my car again. The world just seemed to appear before my eyes and there I was, still driving yet in awe of what just happened, still with a deep sense of peace and love and with an undeniable knowing that I had just experienced God, the truth of my creation, the truth of my identity. I'm still not sure to this day how long I had been unaware of driving or how far I had travelled, for time didn't seem relevant, having just experienced an instant in eternity. And if it took me an eternity to relive that instant, that would be my heart's desire.

In the oneness of God I realised that the truth of our creation is the loving relationship that we all share with one another. This is the meaning of heaven and the knowledge of the universe is contained within this awareness. Beyond the ideas of time and space is where we truly exist. Not as separate, physical beings, but together as the spirit of love in the eternal mind of God.

THE VOICE OF REASON

You are not asked to blindly accept what I have related to you through my experiences and understanding of them. Yes, they are lovely stories filled with mystery and wonder, believable or not. There is nothing special about me. I have no special gift or abilities beyond the average person. I am like you in every way. I possess nothing that we do not share and that is not available to us all. You have the means right now to see and experience the truth as it 'is', for yourself, firsthand, as I have.

You may be put off by statements like 'in the eternal mind of God' or 'knowledge of the universe' or 'beyond the ideas of time and space' or 'the world is an illusion,' believing that they are hollow or without real meaning and could not possibly be experienced or understood. And even if it were possible to understand, what difference would it make to you? Why even bother?

Because it's all about you. It's about understanding who you are and how you function in the world. How do you know anything? How does your mind work and what is it that makes you capable of experiencing life? What is its meaning and its purpose? Do you have a spirit? Are you a creation of God or a product of evolution? What happens after death? It's about who you are right now.

As much as you may believe that you already know everything there is to know about yourself, I'm sure that there are still a few of these questions you have left unanswered. And until you have answered all of these questions you can't really claim to know yourself completely.

It's not necessary to die in order to find the answers, because only life holds the answer to the meaning of life. If you would know yourself, the first step is to make the simple decision that it is something you want to know and as you progress in your understanding of yourself these hollow statements will become filled with your understanding.

REASON

Dictionary definition: *The power of the mind to think, understand, and form judgements logically.*

This is all that is required of you to demonstrate to yourself the basis of your beliefs and opinions and to be able to see things from a different perspective. It has nothing to do with religious beliefs or rituals or whether you believe in God or not. It doesn't matter what your education, race, or situation is. All you need is the willingness to question everything that you now believe about the reality of yourself and the world around you and allow your own logic and reasoning to answer you.

The only honest question is one that you do not know the answer to and if you allow yourself to be open minded to the answer, then you will begin to see differently.

There is a tendency to just dismiss the following ideas as too hard to grasp or perhaps a waste of time with no perceivable outcome or relevance. This is the common response for most, when faced with questions that have never been asked before or have no immediate answer. These questions produce a sense of uncertainty and even seem to attack one's very identity, and so the questions are dismissed and put out of mind.

Be honest with yourself and be open to receiving the answers. They will come and all will make sense if you are willing to just let them, without resistance, but in glad expectation of their coming.

The simple truth is that you are Now who you've always been and always will be and the only need you have is to realise that this is so.

The purpose of the following chapters are to help you to understand the obstacles that stand in the way of your awareness of this simple truth. Each chapter refers to questions I have contemplated about my perceived reality, which seem to be undeniable in the world yet contradict everything that I have experienced in my joining with the truth of who we are.

What is the truth? The truth 'just is' and is beyond worldly description or interpretation. So to understand what 'just is' really means it is necessary to question and bring to reason everything that it is not, so that all that remains in your awareness is simply 'what is'.

LIVING A DREAM

Are you dreaming now or are you awake? Are you sure?

"Of course," you say.

Could it be possible that your wakefulness is only a dream that you are dreaming right now?

"Impossible," you say.

But what if it were true? Would you want to wake up? Or would you prefer to remain asleep and continue living a dream?

We all seem to go through life unaware of ourselves, blindly accepting our lives and the world around us as our reality, never questioning the ideas and concepts that we believe to be true—the ideas that give rise to the illusion of a world that is real and dependable, the world into which we are born and in which we will die being its only certainty.

Sure, it doesn't seem to be a dream whilst you are in it. It is only upon waking that you can see the difference between dreams and reality, for until you are awake you are still dreaming.

DREAMS

Dictionary definitions: *1. A series of thoughts, images and sensations occurring in a person's mind during sleep. 2. A state of mind in which someone is or seems to be unaware of their immediate surroundings. 3. An unrealistic or self-deluding fantasy.*

Let's have a closer look at these dictionary definitions to better understand how it is possible that your life is just a dream.

Think now about what occurs in your sleeping dreams. You close your eyes and after a time your mind becomes still as your thoughts and images and bodily senses subside. All becomes peaceful as all conscious thought of the world and everything in it disappears into nothingness. As you start to dream it would appear that consciousness returns yet in a different form, for your mind would seem to bear witness to the dream without the aid of your body's senses. You see in your dreams without the body's eyes. You can hear in your dreams without the body's ears. You can talk in your dreams without the body's mouth. You can move about without your body's legs and you can think in your dreams without the body's brain. And whilst you are dreaming, the reality of the world as you see it in your waking moments no longer exists.

Whilst dreaming, the laws of the world no longer pertain. Dreams are beyond time and space. They are abstract in content and are without limit or restriction. You may have dreams that you can fly or shapeshift or perhaps you can travel in an instant to places that could only exist in dreams, where nothing is stable or predictable. Sometimes you seem to be the maker of your dreams and sometimes it would seem as if they are beyond your control, as you seem to assume the role of observer or even victim.

Dreams can be good or bad, happy or sad, and most are forgotten almost instantly upon waking as the world takes hold in your perception and now consciousness has shifted back to the confines of the body's senses and you say, "I am awake now."

CONSCIOUSNESS

Dictionary definition: *The state of being aware of and responsive to one's surroundings.*

So what is the difference between sleeping and waking consciousness?

- Whilst you sleep consciousness *is not* confined and limited to the body's senses.
- Whilst you are awake consciousness *is* confined and limited to the body's senses.

But whether you are awake or sleeping, consciousness is still present within your mind and is only limited by the belief that one form of consciousness is more real than the other. You call one a dream and one reality. But think for a moment what your sleeping state and your waking state have in common. In both states you can see and hear and speak and think and move about. In both states there are people and places and situations and events that seem to occur at random. In either state both good, bad, happy, and sad things seem to happen and each state seems to be undeniably real whilst you are in that state. You believe one to be real and the other to be just a dream only because you perceive one seemingly through the body's senses and the other is experienced solely within the awareness of your mind. And you believe that the body is more real than your mind. But isn't it the mind that directs the body? Perhaps awareness itself is your reality, in which you merely dream that you are either awake or sleeping.

There is much more to be said about consciousness, like where does it come from? How does it work? And what does it mean? This will all be explained later on. But first there are a few more things that need to be explored.

With what you now believe, the following ideas may seem unrealistic, even unbelievable. So as you read on you will need to have an open mind as I will attempt to have you demonstrate to yourself beyond a reasonable doubt that you are indeed the creator of the universe and that the world you think you live in is just an illusion, a simple mistake in understanding, a dream you are dreaming.

KNOW THYSELF

Do you know who or what you are?

Do you know yourself completely without a doubt?

When you say 'I am' to describe yourself, what are the words that you attach to this statement?

Listen carefully, because this is who you *think* you are.

The purpose of this section is to help you to begin to realise the true nature of who you are. Here we will examine and question what you now believe about the reality of yourself as you begin to recognise that there is more to you than meets the eye.

So what does it mean to know yourself? To me, knowing yourself is about coming to an understanding of the 'truth' of who, what, and where you are in this very moment. It is the understanding of the statement 'I am'.

YOUR IDENTITY

Firstly, let us examine the most commonly accepted view of reality that underpins the world as we experience it.

The world is a planet that revolves around the sun. In time, the world has evolved to sustain life and through evolution or creation we as humans are born into a world as bodies, separate from the world around us and everything in it, understanding nothing. Born without an established identity, we go through life with our brain interpreting the world through our senses into thoughts and feelings and establishing beliefs about the world around us and who we are and where we fit in.

As children we are frequently asked, "What do you want to be when you grow up?" this introduces the idea that it is possible and in fact necessary to establish an identity for ourselves. As we begin to mature we develop or invent a sense of identity for our bodies based on our projected hopes and desires and through our experiences and beliefs. We grow old and die and then …?

So what is the purpose of your life? To be born into a world with no identity and to go through life trying to create one for yourself so that on your deathbed you can look back and say 'this is what I made of myself' and 'because of what I made my life was like this or like that'? Never realising, that there was never a need to be anything other than who you always were?

You've probably spent your whole life looking for your identity externally, in things like your occupation or roles you play, for example as a mother or father, or in material gains or physical experiences. It would seem that the world holds many opportunities and experiences to help you invent yourself as you try to find your purpose or calling in life. Yet you can only find yourself in the last place you would think to look, for you've hidden yourself well in the belief that you are a body.

The simple truth is that you were not born without an identity. You are now who you've always been and always will be. Your true self cannot be absent from you. It is not obscured, it stands unopposed in plain sight. Yet with your current way of seeing you do not recognise the obvious. So you go through life believing that it is up to you to make something of yourself. Yet you need merely look inward to see the truth of all that you really are, right now.

TRUTH

Dictionary definition: *A fact or a belief that is accepted as true.*

What is the truth?

The dictionary definition would suggest that truth is merely a belief that is accepted as true. It doesn't matter what the belief is, therefore anything can be thought of as true.

For example, if you were asked the question 'what is the truth?' you would probably say, "The truth about what?" You can believe anything is true and call it fact but it doesn't mean that it is.

The word 'truth' is singular in nature. It does not change with different beliefs about what it is, it merely 'is'. It is not defined by your interpretations. It does not change with time nor does your perception establish what it is. It simply 'is'.

It is only through the undoing of the idea of 'truths' (plural), that a singular truth can be realised.

I liken this idea of undoing to the concept of the Where's Wally? books. If you are unfamiliar with these books, they are a form of eye-spy in which Wally, an illustrated character dressed in a red and white striped hat and clothing, is placed somewhere on the page amongst a myriad of objects of a similar size and colour. The objective is to identify where Wally is on the page.

At first glance it would seem that Wally is hidden because his location is not immediately perceived. But Wally is where he has always been on the page, in plain view, yet unseen.

He is not hidden but the other objects on the page seem to obscure him and make him difficult to recognise. As you scan the page you will see many similar objects that are systematically disregarded in your search as you realise that they are not him. Your eyes will go from object to object and through the process of elimination you will finally realise where Wally is and has been all the time, in clear view. And the next time you turn to that same page there is Wally in plain view, everything that hid or obscured Wally has been realised and brought to reason.

As you go through this process of undoing, all that obscures the truth of yourself is seen for what it is or rather for what it isn't. The truth will simply become apparent, for it was never hidden and has always been as it 'is'. There is not really even a process to go through for you are already one with the truth. It only seems to be a process because of your belief in 'truths'.

THE BODY

Dictionary definition: *The physical and mortal aspect of a person as opposed to the soul or spirit.*

Are you only a body or could there be more to you than you think?

Let's have a look at what the body is. Medical science would suggest that the body is a combination of complex organs like the heart and the lungs, the liver, kidneys, stomach, and muscles and veins, etc. Supported by a framework of bones and flesh, they all work in harmony, controlled by the brain that is housed within a head, which contains eyes, ears, a nose, and a mouth. All of these things together make up the body and this is what you are.

Quantum science will tell you that the body and all its workings and attributes are made up of carbon atoms and the body is essentially just 80% water. These atoms combine to form molecules, which come together to form cells, which in turn combine or evolve into organs, resulting in the formation of the body and the brain, and this is what you are. Yet quantum scientists go on further to suggest that as the observed nature of the atom is essentially 99.9999999 empty space, the body really isn't even there and it remains a mystery as to why it can be seen and experienced.

This appearance of a physical body stems from the attachment of 'a body' to the statement 'I am', producing the perception of the illusion that 'I am a body'.

BELIEF

Dictionary definition: *An acceptance that something exists or is true, especially one without proof.*

This is the foundation upon which everything you believe rests: the acceptance that something is true, without proof.

You may not accept this definition and believe that everything you know to be true is in fact the result of what has been proven. But have you ever considered the nature of this proof? In what manner was it proven to you? You may suggest that what you believe has been demonstrated to be true via your body's senses (what you see or hear or feel) and that your physical senses are the only witness to what is real and what can be believed.

Do you think so?

Let's see if this is correct.

- Approximately, what time does the sun rise and set in your part of the world?

Your answer would most likely be a specific time in the morning and a specific time in the evening.

Your experience of morning is in direct relation to the time and the perceived position of the sun. As you go through your day it would seem as if the sun moves across the sky in accordance with the time and eventually disappears over the horizon as it becomes evening. This is your experience every day and so you subconsciously believe that there is in fact a sunrise and a sunset.

But if you think back to your junior science lessons, you were taught that in fact it is the Earth that is rotating as it moves through space. The sun goes nowhere, it does not rise and it does not set. Even though you really know this you still unwittingly choose to believe the contrary and therefore experience the reality of a sun that moves. Therefore you experience the reality of 'what it is you believe' even though it does not exist in reality. This is the manner in which all illusions seem real.

Some may suggest that only what they see is real and is the only hard evidence that can be relied on to determine what the truth is.

So let's see how reliable your eyes are as a witness to what is real.

Scientific and biological studies of how the eyes work have concluded that:

1. The images the eyes see are made up of light or solar radiation reflected from the objects we look at. So what we really see is the reflection of light, not a solid object, as it would seem to be.
2. The observed nature of light is that it is two-dimensional, not three-dimensional as things would appear. It is believed by scientists to be the brain that is responsible for the illusion of depth perception as it does not exist as a reality in itself.
3. Colours are simply a wavelength or frequency of light that is transmitted as electrical signals from the eyes to the brain, where they are translated into colour. So colour is never seen directly as it is merely an interpretation from the brain based on the reflection of light.

So in the belief that what is true is only what there is to see, you must take these three things into account.

All you have, or ever will see, is just a reflection of light. And as it is your mind that interprets this reflection, it must stand to reason that everything you see is but a reflection in your mind. It is only the belief in what you see that makes what is seen believable and everything that you believe to be real and solid and true is merely a reflection of light. Is a reflection real? And if you are mistaken about what it is you see, then logically you must be mistaken about the evidence that establishes what you believe to be true.

The belief that you are a body seems to be undeniable. In every waking moment your whole perception of yourself and the world around you is witnessed to by the body's senses and life apart from your body seems to be incomprehensible, for this is what you believe you are. And whilst you never question this belief, it is impossible to see anything other than through the body's eyes.

The body is the central figure of every dream, and every decision you make is based upon what is of benefit to it. You seek for the body's pleasure with its safety as your main concern and it walks about and talks as if it has a life of its own, autonomous to and apart from your mind and what you think of it. It seems to act and to function of its own accord and its life seems to be sustained separate to and apart from your thoughts.

So, let's see if this is true.

Breathing, for example, is something that seems to occur naturally for the body and requires no thought at all to be maintained. In normal conditions you probably take a breath about every two to three seconds and if it were up to you to consciously think about taking every breath then you probably wouldn't last very long. This would seem to be hard evidence that your body functions by itself, but it is only that you are not conscious or aware of your breathing most of the time that it appears to be so. When you become conscious of your breathing, due to physical activity or shortness of breath, it would appear that you are physically experiencing something that is simply occurring by itself.

Try this next exercise to see if this is so.

- Take a deep breath and hold it. Now you are conscious of your breath.
- Tell yourself that there is no need to breathe again.

Now, still holding your breath, wait and see what happens.

Did your body just start to breathe by itself? Or did you think to yourself *I need to breathe now*?

Breathing is like any other bodily function, it is maintained subconsciously, as is everything your body seems to do. The body is neutral. It does nothing of itself. It can only respond to the mind that directs it.

For example:

- Don't think about moving your hand.
- Now, without your thought, move it.

Can you?

It would seem that your body determines how you will feel and what it is capable of doing and what it can't. You exercise it and pamper it, feed it and entertain it. You send it here and there to seek out what it is you want and its eyes tell you what it sees and its ears tell you what they hear and you believe that you are confined to its senses. You hate it for all of the bad things that it has done in the past and are helpless in the midst of what it may do in the future. And as much as you secretly hate everything about it, you still cling to the hope that someday, somehow it will bring you happiness and that without it you would be nothing and nowhere.

So, let's take a good look at this body that you think you are.

For this exercise you will need a mirror big enough to see your whole body. If this is not possible, then at least big enough to see your whole face.

- Position the mirror or yourself so that you can see your reflection.

What is it that you are actually looking at? Is it your body or a reflection?

Of course it's just a reflection, but is it a reflection of you? Or your body?

- Take a good look into the eyes of this reflection.

Are you compelled to turn away? Or do you like what you see? Why? What sort of person do you think you see?

Have you ever realised that you can never look at your own face or even see your whole body directly? All you ever see is a reflection and it is this reflection that you believe contains your identity, the truth of who and what you are. If you believe that your body is all you really are, it is because you look on your reflection (the unreal) and believe that the truth of yourself can be found in unreality. So, what part of you is interpreting this reflection as you look into its eyes? Is it your mind that tells you what you see? Or is it your body?

Let's further question these beliefs with the aid of some more exercises that will help you to understand yourself from a different perspective.

THE CONCEPT OF SELF

Here we will begin to come to terms with the confusion between who you think you are (I am a …) and who you really are (I am).

THE EGO

Dictionary definition: *A person's sense of self-esteem or self-importance.*

Psychoanalysis: *The part of the mind that mediates between the conscious and the unconscious and is responsible for reality testing and a sense of personal identity.*

The ego is your sense of self, derived from the words you have attached to 'I am'. It is the voice in your head that never shuts up, continually demanding your attention. It is the part of your mind that establishes your beliefs and witnesses to the body's senses. It's where all of your hopes and fears, heartache and pain are held and maintained in your subconscious. It is the part of your mind that creates and maintains the illusion of reality and yet it is nothing more than layer upon layer of unfounded beliefs and imaginary concepts. Derived from illusion, it continually attempts to create an identity for itself, believing that it is necessary, in an attempt to prove its autonomy.

But the ego is nothing, quite literally. It amounts to little more than a mistake in your identity. It is the idea that you are a body that exists autonomously to your mind and is responsible for your interpretation of reality. The ego is simply a point from which to view the world that you have made, and by seeing the world as outside of your mind, you remain unaware that this is not so.

THE VOICE IN YOUR HEAD

In every moment of every waking hour you are quite literally talking to yourself. There is a constant narration that goes on in your head, dictating every detail of your life as you willingly follow its orders and demands, believing everything that it tells you without question. It tells you how you should feel and what you should say, how to behave, and what you must do. You turn to it for advice in every situation and frequently ask it what it thinks of you, which isn't very much according to what it tells you. It keeps reminding you of how weak and lacking and afraid you are. When you look in the mirror it points out all of your faults and imperfections and reminds you of how unworthy you believe you are.

It is to this voice in your head that you unwittingly give control over your every thought and action. And to make sure it is never questioned, it keeps your mind busy and distracted, so there is never an opportunity to. It pretends that it is you by convincing you that its voice is yours, and maintains its disguise by demanding your constant attention. And by constantly giving it, you believe that it is your voice because it is the only sense of self you have ever experienced. So it would seem that there is nothing to question. It is the very same voice that is reading these words to you right now, explaining to you what they mean.

So now, whilst it has your attention, let's ask the one question that it forbids you to ask, the one question that it fears above all else, the answer of which would shatter its disguise and allow you to see who you truly are.

The question is, simply: "What part of me is listening?" What part of you is listening to the voice that is reading these words?

Just let your thoughts be still and wait for the answer.

What did it say to 'you' as 'you' listened?

Maybe something like, "What a stupid question."

Ask the question again, "What part of me is listening" to this voice?

Let your thoughts be still and wait for the answer.

What does it say to 'you' now as 'you' listen?

Probably something like, "I already told you, it's a stupid question."

Ask the question again, "What part of me is listening" to this voice?

Again, let your thoughts be still and wait for the answer.

What does it say to 'you' now as 'you' listen?

Probably something like, "Stop asking the same stupid question. I already told you, now move on."

Ask it again and it may start to become angry.

Ask it again and again and it will probably swear at you and tell you that this whole book is @ #$ % #@ stupid so don't bother reading any more.

It will never answer this question because it doesn't know the answer. But it will do everything in its power to make sure you don't. Its whole existence depends on it.

While it still has your attention, ask it something else, like, "What do you think about so and so?" or "What should I do tomorrow?" I bet there won't be a problem answering these questions.

In every conversation you have with others there is a talker and a listener that seem to be separate and distinct from one another in every aspect. And this is so, even when you are talking to yourself, although it doesn't seem to be. The unquestioned belief that 'they are the same' keeps you from recognising the true nature of yourself, being 'the listener'.

It is in your mind that the talker and listener interact and if they are not the same then you would have to logically conclude that your mind must be split into these two aspects. But mind is 'one' and belongs to the listener. The talker is nothing more than an idea created in the mind of the listener so that there is something to listen to.

It may be the talker that tells you what you hear, but 'you' are the one listening.

In the chapters to come you will often be asked to 'still your thoughts'. This simply means to withdraw your attention and interaction with the voice in your head and to become the listener or observer of your mind. When the narration has stopped and you no longer hear the voice, your mind will be still. It is from this point of stillness that you will come to recognise the difference between the talker and the listener.

There's no point in going into more depth about what the ego is and what the ego does and how it works because in itself it is nothing. Yet whilst you maintain your belief in it, it makes more sense to demonstrate to you what it isn't.

So with this said, have a look at this example that I think best describes the nature of the ego.

Think of the ego as an onion.

Onion

Dictionary definition: *A swollen edible bulb used as a vegetable and composed of several concentric layers.*

If you remove all of the layers, what is left of the onion? What is at the heart of the onion so carefully concealed by its appearance? Absolutely nothing.

Like the onion, the truth of what the ego conceals can only be realised by the removal of its layers, not by examining the layers themselves.

Like the onion, as you begin to remove the ego's layers it would seem that all they contain is what would bring tears to your eyes, and the more you look upon them, the more pain you experience. You are compelled to look away in hope of relief from the pain it causes. Yet at the heart of the onion there is nothing and there can be no cause or effect in nothingness. Yet what conceals this truth is painful indeed. But as each layer falls away you will come closer to the truth of what was always there beyond their concealment, and by doing so you will come to realise that all of your pain came from nothingness. And in this you are free to recognise the truth of yourself as you have been all along.

MY

Dictionary definition: *Belonging to or associated with.*

When you use the term 'my', it would suggest that it is something that belongs to you; for example: 'this is **my** book'. According to the dictionary definition, the statement 'my book' would suggest ownership of it. So, who is it that this book belongs to?

Let's do this exercise to help you realise the illusion of 'my'.

1. Think of the things that you believe belong to you, for example:
   - This is my house.
   - This is my chair.
   - This is my book.
   - This is my computer.

These are just some of the huge list of things that you may associate as belonging to you.

2. Look even closer now at the idea of your physical self and what belongs to you.
   - This is my arm.
   - This is my hand.
   - This is my leg.
   - This is my head.
   - This is my body.

3. Now ask yourself the question, "If all of these things merely belong to me, who is the 'me' that they belong to?"

If they are merely possessions, they cannot be you. They must only belong to you. They are not who you are.

If you lost a leg or an arm, would you still be you? What about if you lost all of your limbs, would you still be you?

"Of course," you say, "they only *belong* to me."

Ok then, what if you lost your head; would you still be you?

"Of course not," you say, "I would be dead."

So then, who is this self that your head belongs to? Or do you think you are a head?

If you can accept that your arms and legs only belong to you and they are not really who you are, then surely reason would suggest the same thing about your head.

If you think that you would no longer exist without a head, it is because you identify with yourself as 'the voice in your head'? This is your sense of self at the moment and you believe that who you are is contained in your brain within your head. But as we just explored, your body merely belongs to you and it is the 'you' that it belongs to that needs to be recognised.

4. Point your index finger at yourself.

Who does it point to? You or your body? What part of yourself does your body belong to?

RECOGNISING YOURSELF

Who do you think you are? (I am …)

- Let's imagine that we are amongst a group of strangers for the very first time and you are asked to introduce yourself to the group.

Who are you?

You would probably start your introduction with the statement 'I am _____' or 'My name is _____'.

This is the basis of your whole identity, your immediate response to the question "Who are you?" Similarly, if somebody called your name from a crowd, you would probably respond as if it were you they were calling.

- Let's now suggest that your name was given to you by your parents and doesn't really have anything to do with who you are. You would still be you with a different name or even with no name at all.

So now, without a name as reference, the same question is asked. Who are you?

What do you say now? At this point of questioning many people are lost for words. Their whole sense of identity rests on their name and many will respond with 'I don't know'.

The most common response from people when asked the question, "Without a name, who are you?" is to tell a story about themselves. For example, their occupations, '**I am** a teacher' or '**I am** a dentist', or the roles they play, like '**I am** a mother or father or wife' and 'I like to do this or that'. This is the way you establish your sense of self. Your perceived identity consists of everything you've learnt and experienced and believe about yourself from the day you were born up until this very moment now.

Well, where is all of this learning and experience that gives you your identity right now? As of this very moment it is all in the past. Where is this past now other than in your mind as a memory? Are you a memory of yourself?

- Now let's suggest that you have no name and that your past has no reality 'now' but only as a memory in your mind.

So right now, with no name and no past reference, who are you?

What do you say now if your name is not who you are, and you are not a memory of yourself?

Some say 'nothing' but you must be something to be able to say 'nothing'.

Some suggest that all that is left is just a body, but if this is correct then what is it that distinguishes you from other bodies? What is it about your body that makes you exclusively you?

Once you have removed the labels that you have attached to 'I am', how do you answer the question, who are you?

The only honest answer would be, "I don't know."

Don't you find it strange that if you ask yourself the question, "Who am I then?" you can answer yourself, "I don't know"?

So who is this self, right here, right now? With no name and no past reference? Who is this self that is unaware of itself?

SELF-AWARENESS

Dictionary definition: *The capacity for introspection and the ability to recognise one's self as an individual, separate from the environment and other individuals.*

This definition pertains to perception and has nothing to do with the awareness of self. It is the belief that both perception and awareness have the same meaning and in doing so makes it difficult to distinguish the difference between them as I will discuss later.

In my understanding, self-awareness refers to what I call 'present consciousness'. It is a state of mind in which you are simply conscious of your thoughts and interactions. It is where your mind is still, not busy with the self-talk that goes on constantly. You become the listener and observer of your thoughts and actions as they occur rather than acting and reacting unconsciously as if on autopilot.

It's not about what it is you are perceiving, it's about being conscious that you *are*.

In a state of present consciousness, where you become the observer of your thoughts, it becomes possible to recognise them as they arise in your mind. As you do so more often, you will come to understand that they come from the part of yourself that is beyond the idea of the body, the aspect of yourself that has no name and no past reference, 'the listener', the 'I am that I am'. From this perspective, life becomes more peaceful and your mind becomes less cluttered.

It may seem like a difficult task to find the time to practice present consciousness (self-awareness) amongst all of your commitments and responsibilities. With so much to think about and plan and do every day, your mind is always occupied and there rarely seems to be a gap in your thinking where your mind is still. So, it's up to you to make one in which it is possible.

MEDITATE

Dictionary definition: *To focus one's mind for a period of time, in silence or with the aid of chanting, for religious or spiritual purposes or as a method of relaxation.*

For some, meditation is thought of as something that monks do, in isolation from the rest of the world in some spiritual temple in the mountains somewhere in Tibet. It may be believed by some that meditation is about long days and countless years of sitting in a particular cross-legged position, trying to come to some sort of spiritual awareness or enlightenment from beyond, while the world goes on without them. But meditation is widely practiced by people from all walks of life as a form of relaxation, whilst for others it is practiced as a means to gain peace of mind or spiritual insight.

The goal of the monk is simply 'to become aware of the true nature of themselves' and they believe that isolation and years of meditation is the way that this is accomplished. But like you, since they've never been separate from themselves all along, sooner or later they must come to realise that this is so. Everybody will come to this same moment of realisation, each in their own way, and although it may seem like a long and difficult journey, it can be shortened immeasurably with the simple decision to just know yourself with the idea 'I would recognise myself as I am now'.

All meditation, regardless of the form you adopt, should start from here if you don't want to waste years only to come to this same point before you can move forward. So the first step in your meditation practice should be directed towards recognising your inner presence, 'the listener'. This is only possible in a mind that is still and so you must learn how to do this.

With little time, yet consistent effort, you will come to recognise and be able to connect with this aspect of yourself.

There is no need to sit in a particular position or to burn incense or to chant obscure words or to isolate yourself in some dark corner. Their purpose is only to enable you to relax and to be free of worldly distraction. They are not necessary, but if you find these things help you to relax and still your mind then use whatever it is that you believe will help you to achieve this state.

There are many meditation techniques available to you via the internet. Some offer a guided meditation or visualisation techniques but I find the most effective way is always the simplest in that it requires little thought in order to practice, with the goal being no thought at all.

The Conscious Breathing Technique

The simplest, most common technique is the 'conscious breathing technique' as all you need do is simply maintain the awareness of your breathing. Since breathing is probably the most natural thing to do, it requires little thought to maintain awareness of it in your mind. Although it still requires some thought, it is singular in nature and presents lack of competition from other thoughts to arise.

- Sit comfortably and close your eyes. Take a few slow, deep breaths and start with the idea 'I would recognise myself as I am now'. Without thinking about what this means, focus your attention on the statement as you repeat it to yourself slowly, several times.
- As you continue to take slow, deep breaths, hold them for about five seconds and then exhale slowly, letting the idea fade from your mind as you now focus only on your breathing as your mind becomes still.

If you find your mind wandering, bring your attention back to your breathing and it will become still again. You may notice a relaxed, peaceful feeling after only several breaths. This is the state of peace in a mind that is still and you will know it is so by this feeling.

This feeling of peace and stillness is where the true nature of yourself can be recognised. The more you allow this feeling to 'just be' what it is, the more you will come to recognise the aspect of yourself that exists beyond the idea of your body. This aspect of yourself is no different from the self you are in every moment of every day. The only difficulty you have in recognising this is the inability to distinguish the difference between the seeming voice in your head and the part of your mind from which this voice comes. And you will only come to recognise this aspect of yourself when your mind is still.

The Data Technique

Another technique I have found rewarding is what I call the 'data technique'. This technique not only results in the stillness of mind but also helps to free your mind from all of your perceived problems and worries and provides a platform for corrected perception.

- Start with the conscious breathing technique as outlined previously, focusing your attention on your breathing.
- Think of your mind as a computer and of your thoughts as merely data; just streams of pointless data. Be the watcher of your thoughts as they come to mind and release them back into the nothingness from where they came. Don't hold on to any one thought as even the idea of data becomes merely data and your mind becomes still.

Practice this idea as often as possible during your day or whenever you are feeling stressed or anxious about anything, for the cause is just meaningless data. Even one to two minutes several times a day will bring results. In these minutes and for some time after, your mind will be quiet and you will be in a state of present consciousness. The more you practice, the easier it gets and the more lasting are its effects.

You may say that it's too difficult to stop your thoughts and the harder you try, the harder it seems. So don't try so hard. The idea is to still your thoughts. If your mind is busy with the thought of making your mind still, then the noise in your mind is maintained by this very attempt. Just relax, don't *try* to make your mind still, just *allow it* to be so.

MINDFULNESS

Dictionary definition: *A mental state achieved by focusing one's awareness on the present moment, while calmly acknowledging and accepting one's feelings, thoughts, and bodily sensations, used as a therapeutic technique.*

This definition of mindfulness would suggest that while focusing on the present moment your mind is still full with thoughts and feelings and the perception of bodily sensations. In other words, your mind is full. Yet the objective of mindfulness in its correct application is to transcend your thoughts and feelings and bodily sensations. If you are acknowledging them, whether calmly or otherwise, then you are thinking about them. This is a form of perception.

Contrary to the dictionary definition, the idea of mindfulness is to bring your attention to the present moment and to refrain from making judgements about anything, simply allowing the moment to 'just be' without your interpretations (thoughts).

This is a form of 'open-eyed' meditation that, for me, naturally followed on from the more widely accepted 'closed-eye' techniques with which I learned how to allow my mind to be still, and from within this stillness to come to the understanding of what it means to 'just be' in the present moment.

Whilst in the state of closed-eye meditation the world and all its distractions are left behind as you embrace the stillness and peace of mind that such practice brings. You come to recognise yourself in a different light and all of your cares and worries are transcended and forgotten. And then you open your eyes and behold the world again, just as you had left it. Its goings on then take preference over your awareness and the peace and stillness of your mind is obscured to you as the distractions of the world take hold again. It would seem that the only way to escape its demands and to be in a state of peace is to close your eyes and withdraw your attention from it, which isn't possible all of the time. Therefore, your peace of mind can only be experienced sometimes.

This used to be my experience, but I came to the conclusion that if I wanted to maintain this state of peace and stillness of mind I experienced in closed-eye meditation then I should find a way to maintain this state amongst the distractions and busy goings on of the world in my open-eyed moments. As I had been practicing meditation for some time I found it easy to still my mind and with some practice I found that I could maintain this state for long periods with my eyes open and with little distraction regardless of what was going on in the world around me. Through the practice of mindfulness, everyday life becomes more peaceful and still as you pay less attention to the voice in your head.

You can try this form of open-eyed meditation but I have found that for it to be beneficial it is first necessary to practice closed-eye techniques until you can successfully reach a state of peace and stillness of mind consistently and without being easily distracted. If you haven't come to this point yet then I would suggest that perhaps you should try the suggested meditation techniques as described earlier before you move on to the practice of mindfulness.

Whatever technique you adopt, meditation will help to bring peace to your life. As your mind becomes still you will see situations and events with more clarity and the meaninglessness of the data will become more apparent and will eventually delete itself. Into this free and unoccupied space in your mind are you more able to recognise the truth of yourself as you are now.

AWARENESS

Dictionary definition: *Knowledge or perception of a situation or fact.*

PERCEPTION

Dictionary definition: *The ability to see, hear, or become aware of something through the senses.*

These definitions both seem to make sense when looked at separately, but seen together they make no sense at all.

For example:

- The definition of perception suggests that it is the ability to become aware through the body's senses.
- The definition of awareness suggests that it is the result of perception.

This infers that perception is the ability to become aware of perception.

What does that even mean?

It is the belief that perception and awareness are the same thing. And by believing so, it would seem that what you perceive is the cause of your awareness, not recognising that it is your awareness that allows you to perceive.

So what part of you is aware of what it is you perceive?

AWARENESS OF SELF

My definition: *The awareness of the self that is aware.*

Now let's look deeper into this self that would be aware of itself, beyond the idea of the body as your accepted identity, to understand the truth behind this illusion.

Try this simple exercise for a different perspective. You will need a blank piece of paper and a pen or marker.

1. Place the blank paper in front of you. Look at it.

This blank paper represents the idea of your true self, pure and clean, timeless and unmarked, the unlimited potential for anything to be written or drawn upon but in itself complete and in need of nothing to be itself. Here you are, the 'I am that I am'.

2. Now get the pen or marker and make a dot anywhere on the paper.

This dot represents your imagined concept of self. Now it would seem that there is something else that exists, something separate and apart from your true self. Now the idea of perception arises, for now it would seem that there is something else to perceive, something that is separate and unlike itself, something that needs interpretation to be understood.

3. Now make another dot on the paper.

This dot represents the attempt of this imagined self to understand how it is separate from itself. With this attempt comes the idea of space.

4. Now draw a line on the paper connecting the dots.

This line represents the idea of distance and direction and also gives rise to the idea of measurement and time.

5. Now put a dot in the centre of, and any distance above, the line, and connect the dots to form a triangle.

Now the idea of shape or form is perceived. Now space and measurement and size and direction and time would seem to exist, giving rise to the illusion of a real world that seems to be separate and outside of you; a world of complexity with its myriad of forms and ideas, mysteries and differences.

Reality has become so fragmented and distorted that we've become lost in the illusion of form and have forgotten the true nature of ourselves being the 'I am that I am'. Now our imagined self seeks to understand itself in the world it made, forgetting that it made it, disguised as consciousness and hidden in the idea of separate bodies.

Now in the belief that it is a separate entity (a body) it attempts to establish its own identity, believing that this is necessary in order to 'be' something. In the search for an identity it continually inserts its own frame of reference by suggesting that 'I am' this or 'I am' that, reinforcing the belief in separation and creating a world to bear witness to it.

6. Now think of the blank page again.

Remember it as it was before you placed your marks upon it, pure and clean, unobscured, timeless and complete, unlimited in potential but in need of nothing to be itself. This is the nature of the statement 'I am'.

So how is it that you don't recognise this truth about yourself?

DISSOCIATION

Dictionary definition: *The action of disconnecting or separating or the state of being disconnected.*

What is separation and the state of being disconnected?

It is an unrecognised state of mind in which you believe in a physical reality and that situations or events exist autonomously to, or outside of what you think, where the idea of cause and effect is reversed. It would seem that the world is the cause of everything that you experience and that you are its effect.

For example: You may believe that something or somebody or some situation can irritate, annoy, or even anger you. You believe that there is something external to yourself that causes you to feel how you do.

It would certainly seem so, but ask yourself these questions:

- Who is it that feels these things? It's you, isn't it?

- Who is it that is thinking these thoughts? It's you, isn't it?
- Whose interpretations of events or situations make you feel a certain way? Yours do, don't they?
- Who then is responsible for these thoughts and feelings? You are, aren't you?

"No, somebody else is responsible for how I feel," you say, "they are the ones who piss me off, it's their fault I feel this way." You accept this belief without question. This is the belief in dissociation, of being separate from the source of your thoughts and feelings, unaware that it is but your own interpretations that affect you. In doing so, you project the blame or responsibility for how you feel onto someone or something else in an attempt to make yourself feel better and free yourself from the responsibility of how you feel.

When you do this you put the solution to your problems and your peace of mind in the hands of who or what it is you projected your blame onto. Now there is no hope of healing because you have disowned the responsibility. Some people can carry their pain with them all of their life, not being able to forgive the one who caused them their sorrows. If only they realised that the cause of their pain belonged solely to them could they find peace and healing in an instant.

Another example of dissociation may include:

- The idea that you can read a person's mind.

If you were asked the question, "Can you read minds?" your answer would most likely be, "No I can't."

However, by dissociation you would say, "That person thinks he knows everything," or, "They think that they are too good to do this or that," or, "They think they can treat me like this."

Well, how is it then that if you can't read minds you know what they are thinking? Through dissociation you believe you can anticipate or interpret what somebody else is thinking. You then accept your interpretations as being the truth of the situation, unaware that you just made it up. Because you can't really read minds. Every time you say 'he thinks' or 'she thinks' or 'they think', this is what you are doing.

Another example is:

- The idea that knowing something has nothing to do with your thinking.

In conversation somebody may say to you, "Do you think so?" and you respond, "I don't think so, I know so!"

Well, how is it that you know so? How is it that you know anything? Don't you need to think about what it is that you would say you know? When you say you know something, it is only what you believe to be true and beliefs are established by and remain as thoughts in your mind, retained in your memory to be called upon in the present and thought of as facts.

These are just some examples, but dissociation gives rise to the whole world and everything in it. It seems as if the world is external to you and that everything you see and feel and experience is the result. These are illusions you believe to be true. Through dissociation you don't recognise that it only exists in your mind. We literally make it up as we go, unaware, for out of mind is out of sight. Dissociation is simply the idea that your thoughts don't belong to you. You attribute their cause to someone or something else, unaware that every thought you have comes from and remains with you. You are solely responsible for how you feel or react and for what you think in any situation and to lay blame on someone or something else is how you maintain this illusion. Every time you say 'because of' or 'she or he did it' or 'it's their fault', this is what you are doing.

THOUGHT

Dictionary definition: *An idea or opinion produced by thinking, or occurring suddenly in the mind.*

Have you ever asked yourself the following questions?

1. What is thought?
2. Where do thoughts come from?
3. What do they mean?
4. Why do thoughts occur when I don't choose them?
5. How can I control them, be aware of them, and stop them?

Ask yourself now and take some time to come to some reasonable conclusions.

Did you get any answers that made sense to you? Maybe?

Let's have a look (in a simplified manner) at how medical science attempts to define thought.

Thoughts are produced by and in the brain by the combination of electrical circuitry, impulses, energy waves, and biochemical reactions with the senses as stimuli. These thoughts are analysed, sorted, and stored in a thing called the mind, which is also a product of the brain. Therefore the mind that thinks your thoughts is an effect of the brain, supported and housed within a body. Also, this would imply that because your thoughts are an effect of or are produced by your brain, then it must logically follow that your brain controls your thoughts and in turn these thoughts dictate your actions, making your brain the dictator of your life and the determiner of what life will be for you.

So, if this explanation is correct, then you can breathe easy, for you really have no control over your thoughts or actions. They will always seem to be random and chaotic and you can never answer these questions because it's up to your brain what you think and you are nothing but the result of what it thinks of you.

Do you really believe this?

Let's go back to the questions and attempt to make some rational sense of them.

1. What is thought?

Thought is the expression of the content of your mind. It is everything that you perceive based on everything you believe. Nothing exists without thought. The reality of the world and everything in it and all that you experience exists 'conceptually' as thoughts in your mind. Thought is the act of creation in which your conceptual thoughts are believed to exist as an autonomous reality (the world). With this belief (dissociation), your thoughts seem as if they are ineffectual and your power to create is reduced to the belief that your thoughts are merely a mechanism for perception and interpretation.

2. Where do thoughts come from?

The answer is simple; from you. "That's obvious," you say, but let's examine this further.

If all of your thoughts are coming from you, then you must be the one who is thinking them. And if you are the thinker of your thoughts, you must be **the thinker before the thoughts**, like the blank sheet of paper as discussed earlier.

3. What do they mean?

Your thoughts mean whatever it is you think they mean. That is their only purpose, their only reality. The only way you can interpret or describe any aspect of anything you perceive in the world or in your life is by thought and therefore it stands to reason that everything can only be just what you think it is. Its reality exists only in your mind, conceptually.

CONCEPTUALLY

Dictionary definition: *In terms of a concept or abstract idea.*

Your life and the world around you would seem to be real and solid beyond a doubt, surely not just merely thoughts?

Try this simple exercise to demonstrate to yourself the validity of this concept.

1. Look around you and focus on an object of your choice. What is it?

2. Now close your eyes and think about something else. What is it?

3. Now with eyes closed again describe the first object whilst thinking solely about the something else.

"I can't do this!" you say. "I need to think about what it is that I would describe."

When you open your eyes is the object still there without you thinking about it? It may seem to be, but are you sure?

4. With your eyes open, focus on the first object again. What is it?

5. Now without thinking about what it is, demonstrate to yourself the reality of the object.

In what manner does it exist if it is independent to and apart from what you think it is?

Let's just pause here for a moment to contemplate this question. Ask it of yourself over and over until you come to a conclusion. Because the answer to this question will be the turning point in your understanding. The answer will be the beginning of a new perspective on life from which you will see more clearly, the simple truth that is before you.

The answer to this question is simple: it doesn't. But this is how 'you' must see it, this is the conclusion that your own logic and reasoning must demonstrate to you for it to be believable and acceptable. There is no other, more complicated answer to be had beyond your comprehension or understanding. It is the simplicity of this realisation that will set your mind free and allow you to truly 'see'.

Back to the questions.

6. Why do thoughts occur when you don't choose them?

They occur simply because most of the time we are unaware of ourselves and the fact that we are thinking all the time. In every moment of every second you are thinking. There is a constant narration that goes on in our minds; "What is this? What does that mean? What will I do next? It's hot. It's cold. I'm hungry. It's not fair. Stand up. Sit down …" and all the other thousands of thoughts that we have every day. Sometimes we are conscious of our thoughts but for most of the time we are just on autopilot, going about our lives acting and reacting, oblivious to the fact that we're thinking at all.

7. How can you control them, be aware of them, and stop them?

There are many ways available in the world to address this last question. There are numerous therapy techniques, counselling services, and even medical solutions that attempt to address these issues. But the common mistake made by many is to reinforce the patient's beliefs in the idea that past cause establishes present conditions, therefore focussing on the healing of effect and not the cause.

A simpler, more helpful solution would be for you to realise that you are the thinker of the thoughts you have. Your interpretations (thoughts) come only from you and mean only what you think they do. You are the thinker of the thoughts you have, therefore you are **the thinker before the thoughts**. From this perspective you realise that you have control over your thoughts and how they make you feel and your power to choose them becomes apparent. No longer are you the victim of past causes and present circumstances beyond your control. No longer are you victim to the outside world and its influences, unless you let yourself think you are.

You choose your thoughts whether you are conscious of them or not and everything you perceive and experience is their result. This understanding is the simple solution to all your problems and worries and the release of all your pain and fears, for they have no reality outside of your present thoughts.

Still not convinced? Repeat the previous exercise steps 1 to 5.

PERCEPTION

Dictionary definition: *The ability to see, hear, or become aware of something through the senses.*

And to who do these senses report to? You or your brain?

Perception would seem to be the ability to interpret or to make sense of your environment through the body's senses in relation to yourself, the perceiver.

Once your interpretations are accepted, they then become a belief and beliefs are then seen as facts. Once you believe something to be fact you say, "It is the truth," you say, "I know," oblivious to the process of how it is that you know anything. Once firmly established in your mind, to question what you believe to be true is seen as an attack because it brings doubt to the stability of your beliefs (an acceptance that something exists or is true, especially one without proof) which must be defended at any cost.

Perception is only concerned with the appearance of form as all form is just an appearance. It doesn't matter what the form is, it can be physical form (what you see, the world around you) or emotional form (how you feel) or mental form (what you think) and what you believe is true will be the form you experience.

Your perception is exclusive to you, as it is the result of what you alone believe and the ways in which you view the world. No two people perceive everything the same way and even though experiences and beliefs can be shared, it would seem that there is no singular truth in the world. Everyone would seem to think differently about just about everything. Even people in the same place and at the same time perceive the same situation as different and in their review of the situation everyone present will have a different story to tell. So what really happened? What is the truth?

Truth cannot be variable, the word is singular by definition, the plural being 'truths', which is merely the result of individual perception. The nature of truth is that it simply 'is'. It's only your perception of what truth is that can be variable.

Because perception is variable, then it must follow that change can occur. Changed perception is in direct relationship to what you think and how you experience things. It is only by comparison that you can perceive the difference in the outcome of situations and events and what makes more sense or is more desirable to you, you will accept. And what is deemed to make less sense or is less desirable will be relinquished, for two opposing beliefs about the same thing cannot co-exist in your perception.

ILLUSION

Dictionary definition: *An instance of wrong or misinterpreted perception of a sensory experience.*

To infer that your perception can be wrong implies that there must be a model of what is 'right' perception. So, who decides what is right and what is wrong? Is the model for right perception simply what seems to be generally accepted by the masses? Is that what makes something true? Wasn't Earth accepted by the masses as being flat at some stage? Did this make it so? No, it was just the result of somebody's imagination accepted as fact and called the truth.

Regardless of where or how your beliefs are derived, their end result is what you accept as true or fact. These so-called facts remain in your memory and become the reference point for your perceptions. They will determine the interpretation for what you see and hear and experience through the body's senses and give the world all the meaning it has for you. You believe that your perceptions are real because you have accepted them as your reality. You generally remain oblivious to and seldom, if ever, question the foundation from which your perceptions came into being and so you look out and say, "This is my reality."

Could it be that reality, as you call it, is just the result of your acceptance and belief in imaginary concepts, like the idea of a sun that rises and sets?

Illusions are the result of the perception of the body's senses. This is illusion in a nutshell. All perception is a misinterpretation because all perception is illusion and although they may seem to be endless in number, one illusion is all illusions and beyond all illusions is the truth, as it always was and has always been.

Remember earlier we discussed that dissociation is an unrecognised state of mind in which you believe that situations or events exist autonomously to, or outside of what you think. This is what maintains the illusion of reality, as you see it, because this is the state in which you simply accept without question this foundation in your beliefs. These beliefs are kept hidden from yourself by projecting them to a world that you believe exists externally to you, unaware that this is what you are doing.

Perception is attributed to the body's senses and so you believe that as you look out on the world, your perception rests on something that exists apart from you and that what is 'actually there' is the cause of what you perceive and that your perception of it is its effect. But although you attribute perception to the body's senses, isn't it your mind that interprets this sensory information by drawing from the beliefs (a function of the mind) that are stored in your memory (a function of the mind) and attempt to make sense of what your perceptions witness by this very process (a function of the mind)?

So, how can it be that the world exists apart from what you think about it?

Without your thoughts, how is perception even possible?

Without your thoughts about what is real, how can you say what is?

Take these questions seriously and look to reason for the answers because until you do you will continue to believe in illusions and they will be all that you will see.

So if all perception is an illusion, then how can you know what is real without it? Good question.

It would seem that everything you know to be true is the result of what you perceive. Yet the truth just 'is' and cannot be perceived. So, it is only through corrected perception that what 'is' becomes apparent.

What is corrected perception? Corrected perception is the undoing of what it is you believe to be real. It is a simple change in perspective that happens by itself when you bring your beliefs to reason and see that you were mistaken. By doing so, you will come to understand that you are the maker of the world you believe (an acceptance that something exists or is true, especially one without proof) to be true. With this realisation, you can see quite clearly that what you once believed to be real was just the fabric of your imagination and, being conceptual, it has no reality and no effects. As your illusions are seen for what they really are, 'nothing', their effects are transcended and no longer perceived. This opens the way to corrected perception, through which all perception is undone and the truth of what just 'is' becomes apparent.

The key to corrected perception is the willingness to be open-minded with regard to everything you believe and perceive. Hold on to no belief that needs to be defended and be determined to see only the truth and you will.

IDEAS

Dictionary definition: *A mental impression.*

IMPRESSION

Dictionary definition: *An idea, feeling, or opinion about something or someone, especially one formed without conscious thought or on the basis of little evidence.*

Ideas and impressions are the basis for what you perceive and believe about everything. They are the means by which the voice in your head establishes your beliefs and opinions, giving the world all the meaning that it has for you. This is the basis from which you believe in your version of reality and call it the truth.

Everything you perceive and believe is simply an idea, a construct of your mind, your imagination, attributed the status of reality through the dissociation of its cause.

An idea is a mental concept at the heart of all human endeavour. In the world everything starts with an idea. It is the seed of all physical form, as an idea becomes action, which then brings about the fruition of the idea into seeming reality. For example, Edison had an idea to create the lightbulb. He then put his ideas into action and finally his idea became reality and his bulbs now light the world.

So imagination takes the form of an idea, which becomes an action, which creates physical form and is then thought of as reality (a thing that exists in fact, having previously only existed in one's mind). And what was conceived in the mind is now perceived by the mind but believed to be separate and autonomous to the mind.

If this is true, then in what manner does anything exist apart from what you think about it?

Where is your imagination? Where do your ideas come from? What directs all of your actions? Where is the perception that would be witness to the result of your actions?

Isn't it in your mind where all of this takes place?

And what exists apart from and outside of your mind? Can you even say anything without thinking? So, why do you believe that what you perceive is no longer just an idea in your mind? Because it doesn't seem to be? Because your mind is just a secondary function of your body?

What do you think about your body? What is it without your thoughts about it? How can you demonstrate its reality beyond what you think about it? Or could it be just an idea too?

What ideas do you have about other people? They seem to be everywhere you look. In your judgement there are good people and bad people. There are ugly people and there are attractive people. There are people that are close to you and strangers that are distant. There are white people and black people, enemies and allies, the fortunate and the unfortunate. Based on your perception of them, you determine who is who and what they mean to you. Most of the time you don't see past their physical appearances as you judge them to be friend or foe and you accept them or reject them accordingly.

But who are they really?

If they are perceived as strangers, then it would be fair to say that you don't really know who they are. But if they are your close friends or loved ones that you spend a lot of time with, then you may believe that you know them well and could accurately describe who they are and what they are like if asked the question.

So let's ask the question.

For the purpose of this exercise, choose the closest person to you, the person who you believe you know the best without a doubt; for example, your wife or husband, your child, a sibling or parent, or a close friend.

It's preferable if this person is present. They don't need to participate, they just need to be in visual range so you can see them clearly.

If this is not possible then use a photograph or bring their image to mind and keep it there as you continue.

- Take a good look at this person in front of you. What role do they play in your life?
- Now without this role of, e.g. husband, daughter, wife, friend—who is it in front of you?
- What is their name?
- Now without their name and the role they play, who is it in front of you?
- What sort of person do you think they are?

- Now without your thoughts about what sort of person they are, without their name and without the role they play, who is it in front of you? Just a body?

If who they are is not solely dependent on what you think about them, then who are they?

When you look at another person, what do you really see apart from your thoughts about them?

Do you still believe you know them well? Not so sure anymore? Is it possible that they are not who you thought they were? Is it possible that you don't really know them at all?

APPEARANCE

Dictionary definition: *The way that someone or something looks.*

Remember, all your eyes ever see is a reflection of light, including other people, and it is your mind that interprets this reflection and shows you what you think about them. Therefore, when you look on other people as you just did, you don't really *see* another person. What you are really seeing is the meaning **you** have given them. The body that you see and believe to be real is just an appearance, projected from within your mind, creating the illusion of a separate person. This is not recognised because you believe that you are a body too and look on other people as you believe you are.

There are no separate people as there appears to be. This doesn't mean that you are alone and that only you exist. Beyond the idea of separate bodies is the 'one mind' we all share and exist within. And it is just an idea in this mind that believes it exists as individual bodies, capable of individual thoughts and of leading an individual life in a world of separation. But this is not so and you will realise this when you come to experience and understand that you but interact with your own mind in every aspect and in every moment. What appears to be other people is just an appearance and nothing else.

To truly see other people, look for what it is that you have in common, not to the differences that would seem to separate you but to what makes you the same. Look on them without judgement and allow them to 'just be' and you will come to see them as they really are and begin to recognise yourself in them.

THE MIND

Dictionary definition: *The element of a person that enables them to be aware of the world and their experiences, to think and feel; the faculty of consciousness and thought.*

For centuries there have been many theories regarding the workings of the mind. Medical science, for example, would suggest that the mind is a product of and contained exclusively within the brain. With the modern technology available today, it is possible to study and measure in more detail the workings of the brain in an attempt to understand it in relation to physical behaviour and cognitive functioning. For example, it is believed that certain regions of the brain are responsible for things like behaviour and emotion, intellect, memory, creativity, motor skills, and all other functions. The electrical circuitry and chemical reactions produced in these regions of the brain are believed to be the cause of all physical and mental functioning.

If this is so then what part of the brain contains the mind?

As the mind cannot be measured or demonstrated through these methods of observation it is concluded, without evidence, that it must be a function of the brain. Since nothing has been discovered to suggest otherwise, it is simply accepted as the place to continue looking until it is. But at least they are honest when they admit that they really don't know how or why the mind exists.

Psychology is the study and analysis of the mind in an attempt to understand its workings, by observing physical behaviour and linking it to thought processes of both a conscious and subconscious nature. Once again, there are many conflicting theories put forward with no proven conclusions. So collectively, the so-called experts of the world all agree that the truth of mind is yet to be discovered and until it is we should just accept without question that it is a product of the brain.

I believe that to understand the mind is to understand yourself, for isn't it you who thinks with this mind? Aren't your thoughts retained as your memories in your mind? Is it not your mind that interprets the world around you and enables you to experience life?

You can never be separate from your mind. Your whole existence depends on it. Every second of every minute of every day, from the moment you believe you were born up until this very moment now, you have been using your mind. Everything you have ever learned and experienced, everything you believe to be true, and everything you see and feel and remember is a function of your mind. Even whilst reading these very words, you are using your mind. Yet we know so little about it and are generally unaware that we are using it at all.

The majority of people leave the mysteries of the mind to the experts to work out and rely on their findings for their understanding.

But most experts look to the brain for their answers, believing that that's where the mind is, as an effect of the brain, obviously unaware that everything they have ever learned and believe and think about the brain is the result of using the very mind that they would try to discover.

After centuries of looking for the mind in the brain, we're still no closer to finding it. So perhaps it's time to think about it from a different perspective. Since it is *your* mind, why leave it to somebody else to tell you what to believe when you can understand it for yourself? It's really just a matter of perspective.

PERSPECTIVE

Dictionary definition: *A particular attitude towards something; a point of view*.

Your perspective is the way you think about something. It is the subtotal of what you believe (an acceptance that something exists or is true, especially one without proof) to be true about what it is that you perceive. It is the *point* from which you look out and view the world and see all the meaning you have given it, unaware that this is so. The result is that the illusion of what you see has a reality of its own, apart from your thoughts, and exists outside of your mind (dissociation).

Simply put, your perspective on the world is the meaning you have given it and the way in which you will experience it. If you believe that the world is frightening and dangerous or unjust and oppressive, this is what the world will seem to be to you. And all that you look upon will seem to bear witness to what it is you believe you see (think about) and experience, because this is the perspective with which you look on the world and believe it to be so.

Yet perspective is not fixed. And even though your perspective on things is the end result of your well-established beliefs and all that you 'know to be true', your beliefs are simply given up and replaced when seen from a different perspective that seems to make more sense.

All that is necessary for this to occur is to be open and willing to see (think about) things differently. Just with the simple idea that 'perhaps there is another way to see things', what you then accept as true will be what you will perceive in the world around you.

Here's a fun example: a riddle in which the only answer is a matter of perspective.

- Three people go shopping for a birthday gift. The selected gift costs $30.00 and it is decided that each person will contribute $10.00 each towards the gift. A $10.00 note is collected from each person to total the $30.00. When they reach the checkout to make their purchase, the cashier informs them that the gift is on sale and now only costs $25.00. Since the $5.00 difference in price cannot be evenly split amongst the three, the cashier suggests that she give each one $1.00 back and that she will hold the other $2.00 as a credit. All agree and as they were about to leave the store, one stopped and said to the others, "Wait a minute. We all gave the cashier $10.00 each for a total of $30.00 and she only gave us each $1.00 back. That means that now we've only spent $9.00 each and if you multiply that by three, that's $27.00 in total and we only got a store credit of $2.00. If you add the two together that's only $29.00 in total. So where's the other dollar?"

You want me to tell you, don't you?

OK then: firstly, you can stop beating yourself up trying to find the missing dollar, because from the customer's perspective this question can never be answered. But if you look at the situation from the cashier's perspective, the question is meaningless.

- The cashier received the purchase price of the goods, which was $25.00. She held a store credit of $2.00 to total $27.00, and gave each customer $1.00 back, totalling $3.00. Added together, the $30.00 has been accounted for, the till balances, and the question is meaningless.

As with this riddle, it is just a simple change of perspective that allows you to see clearly that you were mistaken and that there is indeed another way to see things. Remember that it is you who gives the world all the meaning that it has for you. It has no meaning of itself and all you will ever see in it is from the perspective you have chosen.

DUALISM

Dictionary definition: *A theory or system of thought that regards a domain of reality in terms of two independent principals, especially mind and matter.*

What you believe about your mind determines what your experience will be. For example:

- Does your mind exist within a brain, within a body? (*Matter.*)

- Or does your body exist as a thought within your mind? (*Mind.*)

Both questions are diametrically opposed and which one you choose to believe is simply a matter of perspective, yet one that will determine how you understand yourself and how you experience life.

The belief that **your mind exists within a brain, within a body** gives rise to the world of separation; the belief that there is a world outside of your mind in which situations and events can occur without your involvement or perception and that have no direct relationship to you or what you think (dissociation). This belief would see the mind as limited and weak because it is thought of as a secondary function of the body with no real power to create anything beyond the body that it is dependent upon and confined to.

With this belief it would seem that your thoughts only exist in your head and that they are neutral or causeless unless physically acted upon. It would seem to demonstrate that you are indeed a separate physical being, as you have your own private thoughts just like everybody else. With this belief it would seem that your mind is exclusive to you and is independent of the minds of others.

The belief that **your body exists within your mind** gives rise to a world of inclusion, where there is no separation of mind and all situations and events, the world and everything in it, are understood to only exist conceptually, within your mind. With this idea comes the undoing and relinquishment of dissociation, as you begin to see the truth that you are as unlimited as the mind that encompasses all of creation and that you are joined as one in the same mind that we all share.

There is a well-known quote by the famous philosopher, Rene' Descartes: "I think, therefore I am." This idea would suggest that your very existence, or indeed your very being, is established only by what you think you are. This is true of your imagined, conceptual self.

But if this quote is correct, then who is the one doing the thinking? Where does the ability for conceptual thought come from if you are indeed nothing more than the subtotal of your thoughts? This is clearly a simple case of dissociation, the reversal of cause and effect. However, if you rearrange the words to read 'I am, therefore I think' then the 'I am' would be understood to be the cause and 'I think' would obviously be the effect.

So what statement makes more sense?

- I am the result of my thoughts. ('I think therefore I am'.)
- My thoughts come from who I am. ('I am therefore I think'.)

In the previous section on thought, you did an exercise that demonstrated the idea that what you perceive exists only in your mind as thought and that your perception of reality can only be demonstrated by what you think. With this in mind, which of the above examples makes more sense to you?

Still not sure?

That's OK, most of the ideas presented so far require open-minded contemplation and reasoning before you can accept them as believable. But through the voice of reason, some of these ideas may begin to make more sense to you than the beliefs you have previously held about yourself. It may help, at this stage, to review and contemplate the exercise in which we used the idea of the blank piece of paper to represent your true self to at least come to terms with the idea that maybe your body only exists within your mind.

During my out-of-body experiences, my mind seems to expand or enlarge as it becomes one within an all-encompassing awareness. In this state there is only mind, in which all knowledge of the universe is simply known. In this awareness, reality is understood to be an expression of this mind, the mind that we are all a part of, unified with no separate thoughts, timeless, with no limitation or boundary, complete within itself.

In these next sections we will explore the reality of your perceived environment and the world in which you think you live, and look at some of the unquestioned beliefs you hold about its seeming reality.

THE WORLD

Dictionary definition: *Earth, together with all of its countries and peoples.*

It would seem that no two people ever experience the world in the same way. Perhaps some share common beliefs and experiences, but never will they interpret their meaning in exactly the same way. Each seem to have their own private thoughts about the world and everything they perceive within it and to each one a different interpretation of reality is the result. From this point of view, it could be said that there are over seven billion different versions of the world. So whose interpretation is correct? Yours or mine or someone else's? How real is something that can be interpreted in so many different ways? Logically, it must be conceptual if it has no singular meaning. Yet it would appear that regardless of what others think about the world, your version is what 'really exists in reality'.

Do you believe that the world existed before you were born and will still exist after you die and that your thoughts contribute nothing to its reality?

Let's take a closer look at this idea. What evidence do you rely on to be able to accept this premise?

- You have witnessed the birth of babies into a world that already exists. You were here before they were born and you came into the world just as they did.
- You have witnessed the death of people in the world but you are still here. The world doesn't disappear when they die and you will die just like them.

It seems like hard evidence, doesn't it?

But look at your reasoning from a different perspective.

1. You **perceive** (a function of mind) that babies are born into a world that already exists. And you **remember** (a function of mind) that you were once a baby.
2. You **believe** (a function of mind) that people die. And you **expect** (a function of mind) to die just like them. You **believe** (a function of mind) that the world will still exist after you are gone.

And none of this has anything to do with what you **think** (a function of mind) does it?

The world is just an appearance, created by you, in your mind. You can only **perceive** or **remember** or **expect** or **interpret** or **know** or **think** or **believe** that the world is real and exists apart from and separate to your mind and what you **think** about it, whether you **believe** this to be true or not.

So with this said, why does the world still seem so real?

Because every second of every minute of every day you are **thinking** about it. Yet it is only your **thoughts** about its reality that would make it seem real.

So if the world is not real ... then what is?

Simply, just the mind that thinks the world is real. And that is the only reality that the seven billion versions of the world share, the only singular truth to be found in the world.

Think about what takes place in a movie theatre.

- A movie is projected onto a screen and you, the audience, view the images that are being projected.
- As you had nothing to do with the making of the movie, you sit in anticipation of what will unfold before your eyes.
- The projector shines the light containing the images, which appear on the screen. This light is then reflected back to the eyes of the beholder, you the audience.
- From your place in the audience, your eyes see this reflection of light and your mind interprets this reflection as images and gives them meaning while you sit and watch the movie. Yet, unaware of this, you believe that it is the images you see that hold their own meaning.

And so it would seem that this is the way in which you experience the world.

- As you believe that you had nothing to do with the making of the world and all its happenings, you believe that you are a part of the audience.
- You see the world from your position in the audience (where your body is) and look at the images on the screen before you (the world).
- And it would appear as if it were the images themselves which contain all of the meaning you see.

From this perspective it would seem that the world is very similar to a movie, in that you are merely a part of the audience, with no say in what it is you will behold and with absolutely no power to change the script as it unfolds in time. From this perspective the world does indeed seem to be real and meaningful, separate to you and existing independently to what you think about it.

So let's look at your contribution to the movie that seems so real.

- The movie (your life) is conceived of, scripted, edited, filmed, and produced in your mind before its release.
- The projector (your mind) projects the images to the screen (the world you believe you see).
- From your place in time and space (the belief you are a body) you look out on the world you have projected within your mind and see the reflection of your thoughts, believing that the

appearance of the reflection is that which is real. And so it is to you because you do not recognise that you are the maker of the movie.

- You are the star, the world is your set. You play the role of hero or villain, the slayer or the slain, the innocent or the guilty. You are the scriptwriter, the director, and the producer. You choose the location and assign the roles for all of the actors and extras in your movie, making sure that your script is followed precisely. Regardless of the theme of the movie the title is always *The World, According To Me*.

If you don't like the movie that you are watching, there's no point banging on the screen in the hope that it will show you something else.

The only way to change the movie is from the point of projection; your mind. Since it is you that writes the script, you can change it at any moment.

What about nature and all of its aspects? What about the wind and the rain, the land and the oceans, and all of the animals great and small that inhabit the world and interact with each other without your participation? Surely their very existence would demonstrate that the world has its own reality beyond your thoughts?

With the belief that your mind is contained within your brain, how could it be suggested that your weak and limited mind could merely think them into existence?

Try this exercise.

1. Don't think about what exists in nature.
2. Now describe what it is that exists.

Nature is like any other aspect of the world. It is only an appearance, simply a reflection of the mind accorded reality by dissociation. And whilst you are content with believing that you are just a part of the audience (a body), you will never realise that it is you who are the movie maker.

How can you recognise that this is so?

Think of the world and everything you perceive within it as simply just an idea (a function of your mind). This much you should have already demonstrated to yourself through the exercises that asked you to demonstrate reality without your thoughts. Realising that you can't do this, you must have come to the logical conclusion that this much is true. Although it doesn't really seem to be.

Your belief that your mind exists within your brain, within your body, would seem to oppose this logical conclusion because you believe your thoughts to be ineffectual and weak. You believe that they have no power to do anything of themselves and that your strength comes from your body and it is only your body that can demonstrate reality and you are limited by its abilities and frailty. From this perspective you conclude that your mind is merely a function of this weak and limited body, incapable of creating an illusion of a world so seemingly real.

But if you can logically accept that reality cannot be demonstrated without thought, then the next logical conclusion must be that since your thoughts are a product of your mind then it must be your mind that contains your thoughts of the world. The acceptance of this simple, rational, logical conclusion is the turning point in understanding from which you will begin to recognise that you are not a body of flesh and bone but that you are mind and spirit. From this perspective, reason will show you that the world is indeed just thoughts projected in your mind and you will understand how it is that you are the movie maker.

THE ILLUSION OF TIME

Dictionary definition, TIME: *The indefinite continued progress of existence and events in the past, present, and future regarded as a whole.*

We all seem to go through time; day after day, year by year, constantly reinforcing its reality in our minds as we organise every moment according to its laws and constraints. As children we begin to learn and accept the reality of time and then go on to demonstrate its reality to ourselves by living our lives accordingly. From birth to death we seem to go through time, accepting its reality without question.

So, let's ask the question; what is time?

Time is a shared idea/concept that enables society to function in an orderly manner, enabling us to plan and organise our lives.

Time is a form of measurement that stems from the observation of the Earth's rotation and orbit around the sun (motion). The method used by scientists to establish or to keep time is to expose an atom to energy, which in turn makes the atom vibrate at a rate of 1/10 billionth of a second. On the last ten billionth vibration it then becomes the next second. This keeps time accurate to the second for over one million years.

The idea of linear time incorporates three elements:

Past > > > > Present > > > > Future

This idea suggests that life progresses through time from the past to the present to the future. From this perspective it would seem that 'past cause' establishes 'present conditions', which influence 'future outcomes'.

THE PRESENT MOMENT (NOW)

Dictionary definition: *The period of time now occurring.*

Using the present (now) as the reference point, let's examine the reality of time. From this present moment the past is gone and its only reality exists in your mind as a memory. The future is yet to come and its only reality exists in your mind as an expectation. So then reason would suggest that from this present moment, both the past and the future exist only as thoughts in your mind. They have no reality **now**. The past can only be remembered **now**, the future can only be anticipated **now**.

Try this exercise to demonstrate this idea to yourself.

1. Sit quietly and slowly look about yourself without focusing on anything in particular.
2. Bring your attention to this very moment, **now**.
3. Ask yourself the question, "Where is everything that I have ever experienced in my life, right now?"
4. Look around yourself. What do you see? Can you see any of this experience now?

Can you physically see anything happening prior to this very moment? Where is the whole day you just experienced, the last hour and everything you did in that hour?

It's nowhere, it's just a memory in your mind. You can perhaps see the result of something that you believe you did in your day but you can only see it now.

So how long, in the idea of time, is the present moment or now?

According to the measurement of time, less than 1/10 billionth of a second, and if time's measure was 1/10 trillionth of a second then the present moment would then be less than 1/10 trillionth of a second and so on and so on. Because it is impossible to perceive anything at this rate, how is it possible that you seem to be able to experience the present moment? Even as you are reading these words it would seem apparent that you are consciously perceiving this moment, but according to the measurement of time the present is less than 1/10 billionth of a second; too fast to perceive.

- Do you perceive the present from the viewpoint of the past? How can this be if the past no longer exists once the future leaves the present in less than 1/10 billionth of a second?
- Or do you perceive the present from the viewpoint of the future? How can this be? For the future is not manifest until it becomes the present in less than 1/10 billionth of a second, and then it is the past.

If you are conscious of the present moment now, then is it the flow of time that you perceive?

The concept of linear time suggests that time flows from the past to the present to the future. But how can the past unfold in the present?

Isn't it the future that seems to unfold in the present which then becomes the past?

From this perspective, simple reasoning would suggest that the idea of linear time makes no sense and in perception the reverse is experienced in that the flow of time seems to be:

Future > > > > Present > > > > Past

So do you progress from the past into the future or does the future proceed to the past?

Regardless of which direction you accept as being the flow of time, it is only in the present moment (now) that the seeming reality of time can be perceived. The idea of a past that extends to the future is nothing more than the misguided belief that past cause establishes present effects.

Remember, time as we know it is just an idea, a measurement of motion, a man-made concept. We've been taught to accept its reality and we believe that it is real and live our lives within its accepted reality, which is firmly established in our minds. It is only through questioning the reality of time that we begin to see that its whole foundation is based on misperception.

THE PAST

Dictionary definition: *Gone by in time and no longer.*

Where is the past? Gone by in time (nowhere). What is the past? No longer (nothing).

The idea of the past is just another form of dissociation. The past has gone by in time and no longer exists but what you fail to recognise, by dissociation, is that you really do believe that it still exists.

"No I don't," you say. "It's easily understood that the past is no more."

Is it?

Then how do you know what anything is? How do you know what a tree is, or a dog or a house or water or a car or a mountain? How do you know how to walk or talk? How is it you understand anything? Isn't everything you know the end result of all your learning and experience from the day you were born up until this very moment? Well, isn't that all in your past, now?

It would seem that without your past learning you wouldn't be able to understand anything in the present moment, for you would have no reference from which to base your understanding.

What is the general theme of the conversations you have with other people? Aren't they about the things that you did in the past?

Do your conversations include opening statements like 'I went', 'I did', 'I had', 'I used to', and 'I remember when'? These are all past tense statements that you continue to describe as if they have some sort of relevance to the present. If your mind wasn't constantly drawing from your experience and interpretations from the past, if it was really understood as *gone by in time and no longer*, then what would the theme of your conversations be? What would you really have to say about the present with no past reference? Probably something like 'I will', 'I should', 'I'm going to', 'I shall', and now your thoughts go from the past to the future. The present moment is almost always overlooked as your thoughts constantly vacillate between the past and the future, but it is only in the present that you can think of either.

In the world it is common practice to look to the past, in the hope of understanding the present, in the belief that present effects are established by past cause.

Through science we look back over billions of years to come up with the big bang *theory* in an attempt to explain the creation of the universe. But it is only through present observation that the universe can be perceived. The past is *gone by in time and no longer*, it has no reality now. It cannot be perceived or experienced now. Any evidence of past cause is nothing more than the belief (an acceptance that something exists or is true, especially one without proof) that this is possible.

THEORY

Dictionary definition: *A supposition or a **system of ideas** intended to explain something, especially one based on general principles independent of the thing to be explained.*

For example, Darwin's **theory** of evolution.

The **idea** (an opinion or belief) of evolution looks to past cause in order to explain the present condition of life as we believe it to be. It would seem that the **evidence** (the available body of facts or information indicating whether a belief or proposition is true or valid) is abundant. Yet this so-called evidence is really nothing more than the result of the **belief in the idea** attributed the status of **truth** (a fact or belief that is accepted as true). As compelling as it may seem, the evidence that past cause establishes present effects is the subconscious denial that the past is *gone by in time and no longer*. Even though you believe that you have accepted that the past is no more, it would still seem to be a reliable source when it comes to making sense of the present.

THE FUTURE

Dictionary definition: *Events that will or are likely to happen in time to come.*

The belief in a future that is yet to come is the idea that something beyond yourself has the potential to manifest itself in reality. It lays dormant, unwritten until the moment in time that it presents itself. You think you can plan for its coming, you set goals with the idea that in the future you will somehow be better off than you find yourself at present. But plan and hope as you may, it would seem that you have no control over what will happen or the form it will take. It seems to have an existence of its own and is entwined in some sort of pre-determined destiny, a mystery that unfolds before you, beyond your understanding. There is nothing you can do to prevent its coming and with a bit of luck it will bring with it your hopes and desires. But there is always the underlying fear that it may bring disappointment and that you may find yourself worse off than before.

We buy insurance to offset the financial expenses if disaster strikes, as we attempt to predict events and circumstances that we simply imagine and then believe could possibly occur.

Like the past, the future can only be thought of now and whatever you think about it is nothing more than your present imagination and projected expectations, as the future has no reality of itself.

What do you imagine the future holds for you?

• Count off five seconds.

Are you in the future or is it still now?

Another accepted concept of time is the idea of time zones. The time zone is the idea that at this very moment now, the time in just about every country in the world is different. This means that everybody's experience of the concept of time is variable.

If time is real then there can be only one aspect of time. If it can be broken up and made different in experience and perception depending on where you find yourself in the world, doesn't reason suggest that the only reality time has is the version you believe in and accept as true?

What about daylight savings, where time is simply added or subtracted by setting your clock forward or backwards, the result being an adjusted perception and experience of time?

If you look to the future in hope of finding happiness or love or peace or your purpose in life or anything that you lack in this moment, it will never be realised, for you are looking where these things can never be found and disappointment will be all you will find. Don't waste another moment hoping for future happiness, just look to now.

The future is always *yet to come* by definition. Tomorrow never comes. If it did then you could no longer call it tomorrow, and when it 'seems' to come it will still be now.

SEEING THROUGH THE EYES OF TIME

Whilst you look to time to find meaning in the world, you will not see that it is you who gives it all the meaning that it has. Through the eyes of time is cause and effect reversed, creating the illusion of a reality that seems to bear witness to itself. Its evidence seems to be undeniable and is beyond any question or doubt as you perceive nothing contrary to what it is you believe to be real through its eyes. As you look back through history it would seem that past cause is very much a part of your present condition.

For example:

- You believe that if it weren't for your ancestors you wouldn't exist in this time that you find yourself in.
- If it weren't for the scientific endeavours of the past there would be no present technology that allows you to live as you do.

- If there was no cause from the past then there would be no present and no future.

When you look to time to find evidence of time, you cannot but find the evidence that you seek because what you see is always the result of what you believe can be found. Because time is your point of reference, what could you expect to find but the result of that which is referenced?

To understand this more clearly, let's use simple mathematics to draw an example. Simple addition can use the symbol (+) to establish what more than 1 means. For example, $1 + 1 = 2$. In this equation (+) is the operation or point of reference from which the answer of 2 is derived. But if there is no reference (+) then all you have is a 1 and a 1, which equals nothing without it. Without the reference (+) there is no equation as it is only the reference that makes the equation seem possible.

Time is a matter of perspective and if you would see past the illusion of time then you must change your point of reference.

TIMELESSNESS

Dictionary definition: *Not affected by the passage of time.*

So if there is no time, then what is there? Simply timelessness, simply just this moment right now. It is only in this moment right now beyond the concept of time that you can truly know yourself. For the very nature of yourself is timeless and can be neither sought nor found within the idea of time.

ETERNITY

Dictionary definition: *A state in which time has no application; timelessness [the encounter between time and eternity].*

The encounter between time and eternity is the birth of the belief in time, as we understand it to be. Remember, eternity has no beginning and no ending and is always now. Time is simply the idea that there can be a point in eternity from which it is possible to look forwards or backwards. This idea creates the illusion of the flow of time, which is believed to extend from past to present to future even though it is the reverse that is experienced in perception. The preoccupation of your thoughts with the past and future maintain the illusion of the flow of time, until you realise that you can only think of either now (a state in which time has no application). This encounter between time and eternity is just an idea that you have learnt to accept as true, without question. In doing so, you believe that time is real and that its effects can be experienced.

So how can you experience timelessness? Simply by letting go of the idea of time. How?

- Just still your mind and bring your attention to this very moment with the idea that now is all there is. It's not about what's happening in the moment but the moment in which it is happening.
- Tell yourself, "There is only now. What will I think next?" Just wait in silence, as the observer of the next thought that comes to mind.

In that moment between thoughts there is a stillness in your mind, a pause from where the next thought would emerge. This pause is timelessness itself, where nothing is yet written; a pause in the idea of time where there is no beginning and no end; a tiny space where you are free from everything the world would seem to demand of you; a tiny space where you are free from all your problems and worries; a place of safety where nothing is happening and nothing has happened. This place is where the truth of yourself can be recognised and experienced.

You may say, "This exercise is all well and good for what it brings in the moment but life goes on and I still need to function in the idea of time to continue living in the world." This is a reasonable statement. For although you may accept the idea of timelessness, how can you incorporate this idea into your everyday life?

Simply, whenever you have a quiet moment in your day, just still your thoughts and bring your mind to the idea of now. Whenever you have a problem or need to make a decision or are feeling angry or sad, bring it to this moment now and you will see it for what it is.

Think, for a moment, about what must be true if there is no time.

- If there is no time then there never was or will be a time that you were less than perfect, could be different, suffer loss, or could be anything more than you are right now.
- If there is no time then there never was a time that anything you ever did, or remember, really happened at all.
- If there is no time then there never was a time that you were born into a body or a time in which it will die.

- If there is no time then there never was a time that the world was created or a time in which it will end.

If time is real and not just an idea, then none of the above can be true. If time is not real, then all of the above must be.

The more frequently you bring your attention to now, the more apparent it becomes and the longer this state of timelessness is experienced. As you carry with you its effects, life becomes more peaceful and the awareness of your true self begins to emerge. With the letting go of the idea of time, all your hurt and pain and scars from the past are transcended as you simply realise that the past is *gone by in time and no longer.* All of your fears and worries and disappointments will cease to exist as you simply realise that the future is but imagined. And peace will come to envelop the mind that is free of the idea of time. Make this your point of reference, from which the illusion of time is transcended.

There was a moment in my practice of 'present consciousness' where, once again, I found myself beyond the perception of my body. As my awareness enlarged, it was as if I found myself far above Earth in a state of timelessness where all was still. Images of the world seemed to flash in my mind as if I was watching a film clip about the flow of time, with the images of a world changing from ancient times to modern civilisation. The world and all its changes and events were understood as being merely illusion, just an idea with no meaning or effect on the eternal nature of reality.

It's hard to describe these moments of 'revelation', as I call them. During these moments, the images that I become aware of are encompassed by a complete understanding of what they mean. It's as if there is an all pervasive, unquestionable knowing that I become a part of, a knowledge that seems all so familiar, as if I was simply remembering what I already knew, yet had forgotten.

THE ILLUSION OF SPACE

Dictionary definition, SPACE: *A continuous area or expanse that is free, available, or unoccupied.*

Space is a seemingly endless void, or nothingness that surrounds and defines all form.

For time to exist, so must space, because time is the measure of motion in space. The orbit of Earth around the sun is only possible if there is space for the Earth to move in. How long does it take for the Earth to move through space, around the sun? 365 days, and that is the basis of the measurement of motion in space. So without space there can be no motion or measurement of time.

As we just explored, time is only an idea, a man-made concept. So could it be possible that space is just an idea too, being like time, just a learnt concept accepted without question?

You may think of space as outer-space, beyond the world you live in, where the planets and stars are. But what about the space that you move about in, in every minute of every day? What about the space that appears to surround you right now, separating you from everything else in the world; the space that defines all form? How would you distinguish one object from the next if not by the space that surrounds it, by the space that seems to separate everything we see?

How do our eyes see space?

They don't. Remember, the eyes only see two-dimensional light. Space, or depth perception as it is referred to, is a mental construct according to those who study the eyes and the brain. Yet it still seems to have a reality of its own as something that can be seen and experienced.

What is space made of?

Logically, you would have to say, 'nothing'. According to the dictionary definition, it is just an *area that is free or unoccupied*. So space is essentially nothing, made of nothing, that contains nothing.

How is it that you can see and experience nothing and believe it contains something?

Let's explore what science believes about the reality of space.

Just to make it clear, I am not a physicist of any sort and my understanding of the dynamics of quantum theory, as it is accepted, is perhaps little more than basic even after countless hours of self-study.

QUANTUM MECHANICS

Dictionary definition: *The branch of mechanics that deals with the mathematical description of the motion and interaction of subatomic particles.*

This is the study of the particles of energy that define the makeup of an atom. Atoms are believed to be the building blocks of all matter. Atoms group to form molecules and molecules group to form all elements that make up the world as we perceive it. From this perspective everything (all form) is essentially just particles of energy that exist in space. The world seems to be solid and real but at its most fundamental level it is just energy and space, with space being the main component of the atom. For example, if it were possible to enlarge the nucleus of an atom to the size of a basketball then the nearest electron particle would be over twenty miles away from the nucleus or centre of the atom. This means that an atom consists of approximately 0.0000001% energy and 99.9999999% empty space, which is what makes up the world as we see it.

So what does this all mean? In a nutshell, it would suggest that the world around us is not really as solid and as stable as we perceive it to be. All physical form is essentially illusory and is little more than empty space. Just empty space in which we perceive the world through the eyes of the empty space that makes up the body we call ourselves.

Due to the scientific conclusion that all form is fundamentally nothing, scientists are currently spending millions of dollars to research the theory that space isn't really nothing after all and that nothing is really something at the quantum level. And so the search continues to find something in nothing so that the something can be reduced to nothing once more, in an attempt to understand it.

Time and space are the same illusion. They are just ideas, concepts that we accept without question, with our belief in their reality being the only reality they have.

What would there be if there was no space?

Simply stated, everything would be one. There would be no separation or gap between you and everything that is. Everything would be recognised as a part of you for there would be no means of comparison to distinguish yourself from anything else. There would be no place to go, for you would be everywhere. There would be no need to be any one thing as you would be everything. There could be no lack or loss or gain because you would have everything. If there was no space and no time then you would be and have everything right now and so it is.

Try this exercise in spatial awareness.

1. Look slowly around you, see the space that surrounds everything.
2. Focus your attention on the space that surrounds each object you look at.
3. Now bring your attention to the space that surrounds you.
4. Contemplate what you would experience if there was no space between you and everything that you see; the idea that you are one with everything (not in body but in mind).

Through the practice of 'present consciousness' it becomes easier to bring your mind to a state of stillness; the stillness that precedes all thought and doing. This is where you can recognise yourself as **the thinker before the thought,** the 'I am' from where all thought precedes. From this perspective you will come to understand the illusory nature of your belief in time and space as your own reasoning leads you to the truth.

THE NATURE OF FORM

Dictionary definition, FORM: *The visible shape or configuration of something.*

Philosophy: *The essential nature of a species or thing, especially (in Plato's thought) regarded as an abstract idea which real things imitate or participate in.*

In the microscopic world of the atom it has been observed that all is seeming chaos. Nothing is stable. Subatomic particles seem to exist at random as they come in and out of existence in time and space, behave unpredictably, and can even exist in many places at once. Even the outcome of the same experiments conducted at this level are not consistent as the observer's expectations seem to influence their outcome. This leads to the question posed by scientists and physicists: why does form appear to be stable and predictable in mass (large groups of atoms) when at its most fundamental level it is seemingly random and chaotic?

Science endeavours to understand creation through the act of separation. It looks to its smallest parts in search of the understanding of the whole. Form is dissected over and over again until its parts become too small to observe and measure.

The reality of form, as it is thought to be, has been theorised and demonstrated and mathematically formulated to the point where the answer to creation would seem to exist in nothingness. In this conclusion, they are absolutely correct. This simple conclusion would seem to finally hold the answer to creation but as it cannot be reconciled in terms of perception it would seem that there must still be more to be understood.

The absolute power of the mind is depreciated by the belief that matter or form has its own reality or intelligence that exists autonomously to the mind. The mind is still thought of as very much a mystery and is simply accepted as being just an effect of the brain, even though there is no evidence that this is true. The reversal of cause and effect is the direct result of this belief as form is seen to be the cause and the mind is thought to be the effect.

I find it peculiar that well-learned, committed scientists who would derive all of their research and theory from concrete evidence and proven facts simply accept, with no proof at all, that the mind is an effect of the brain, and by doing so they look to effect in the attempt to understand cause. Yet, they remain perplexed as to why they can't explain creation. It's like trying to conduct an experiment with no understanding of the equipment you are using. What results could you hope for?

Since it is through perception that the universe is experienced, surely it would make more sense to explore the origin of perception. As a result, perception and creation would be reconciled in a singular truth that holds the answer to both. By using the brain as the point of reference to understand the mind, the answer will continue to remain elusive.

Why does form appear to be stable and predictable in mass when at its most fundamental level it is seemingly random and chaotic?

The simple recognition of memory and expectation as the catalyst for the perception of form seems to be overlooked by physicists in their quest to find the answer to this question. But once again it is just a simple matter of perspective.

For example:

- Place an object in front of you in plain view.

This object is said to be comprised of billions of atoms, random and chaotic in nature as its particles come in and out of existence in time and space. As you look at the object it seems quite stable. It's just sitting there in front of you. It doesn't disappear or change shape or form. It doesn't move through time and space. It's just there.

- Now pick up the object and place it out of sight.

What has just happened?

The atoms that are said to make up the object have now moved through time and space and have now become non-existent.

"No it didn't," you say, "I just picked it up and moved it from one place to another and it still exists."

Does it? How do you know where it is now? Isn't it because you remember where you put it? Did you observe atoms moving through time and space?

"No," you say.

Well, what is the object made of and how far out of sight did you put it and how long did it take you to put it there?

Let's look at it again.

You picked up a handful of atoms (the object) with your hand (which consists only of atoms) and moved them through space (point A to point B) and this took some time to do, how long depending on the distance of the movement. Now, when the object is out of sight, your only reference to its existence is your memory of moving the object and the expectation that it will still be where you remember putting it.

You may suggest that the object still exists without your perception of it, but what evidence do you really have beyond your **belief** (an acceptance that something exists or is true, especially one without proof) that it does?

You can only verify the existence of the object through the act of 'intentional observation' (perception). So, until this point, you have absolutely no evidence that it still exists. Your memory of moving the object and your expectation that it will still be there are the only evidence you have. This is what creates the illusion of reality beyond perception, or in other words, a world that exists beyond your immediate perception of it.

You only perceive what it is you believe, and if you can't perceive it you can only believe it.

So you just made atoms move through time and space and even rendered them non-existent, and you did all of this with your mind. How?

It was your mind from where the thought came that instructed your arm to pick up the object. From this same mind came the decision of where to place the object and the instruction to your arm to place the object where you believed it would be out of sight; all of these actions were conceived and perceived in the same mind that directed them.

You may say, "I didn't move the object with my mind, I physically moved it."

If that is so, then without thinking about picking the object up and moving it, pick it up and move it. Can you?

The observed nature of the atom doesn't behave any differently in mass. It is always random and chaotic and is continually coming in and out of existence and moving through time and space.

SCHRODINGER'S CAT

Schrodinger's cat is a thought experiment sometimes described as a paradox, devised by Austrian physicist Erwin Schrodinger in 1935. This scenario presents the idea of a cat that may be both alive and dead simultaneously, with this state being tied to an earlier random event.

A cat, a flask of poison, and a radioactive source are placed in a sealed box. If an internal monitor detects radioactivity (i.e. a single atom decaying), the flask is shattered, releasing the poison that kills the cat. When the observer looks in the box the cat is seen as *either* alive or dead, not both alive and dead at the same time. This poses the question of when exactly does reality collapse into one possibility or the other. This experiment can be interpreted to mean that while the box is closed, both possibilities exist simultaneously, and only when the box is opened and an observation made does the state of the cat become manifest in perception.

If this paradox is true in the observation of the state of the cat, then it must also be true of the existence of the cat itself.

For example: both the cat and the poison exist and do not exist simultaneously. For it is only through the observation of the contents of the box that the cat and the poison become manifest in perception, as well as the state of the cat being alive or dead. The belief that the cat and the poison are still in the box once it is closed, is due only to the memory and expectation of the one conducting the experiment. Once the box is closed and the contents are no longer perceived, all that exists is potential. It is only the belief that the cat and the poison still exist in the box once closed that would give rise to the possibility of observing the state of the cat.

There are many other theories derived from this paradox; all endeavour to answer the questions of **when** and **how** does physical reality (form) come into existence. But there is no need to theorise; simple logic and reason hold the answer. In fact, the answer is so simple that it seems to go unnoticed in the effort to find a more complex mathematical solution through the process of self-reference as discussed earlier.

The answer is really just a simple matter of perspective, which is demonstrated in every moment and can be understood now.

WHEN AND HOW DOES PHYSICAL REALITY (FORM) COME INTO EXISTENCE?

When?

Form doesn't come into existence. It is merely conceptual, an appearance, a reflection of light, assigned present reality by your subconscious memories and expectations that gives form its appearance of stability and reality.

For example:

- Think of the location of an object that you believe exists outside of your immediate perception.

This could be, say, a pair of socks in a sock drawer or your toothbrush in the bathroom. You believe that the object is where it is only because you remember where you put it and you expect it to still be there. This is confirmation in your mind that it still exists apart from your perception. But right now, it is beyond your sense perception. So you can't really know it is there. You can only suggest that it is. Its existence can only be confirmed by observation or sense perception and this is the paradox that suggests that existence/reality only becomes manifest upon observation, which until this point is only potential.

How?

Form is conceived and perceived in the mind and is seemingly projected outward from its point of reference (the idea of body).

For example:

- Focus your attention on an object (form). What do you see?
- Does the object appear to be within your line of vision, separated by the space between you?
- Do your thoughts about what it is you see enable you to label it?
- Can you label it without your thoughts about what it is?
- Where are your thoughts coming from? Are they a function of your mind?
- What is your point of reference from which you perceive the object? Is it your body's eyes? Or is it your mind that perceives the object?

All form, being the world and everything in it, is just an idea, it is conceptual, conceived and perceived and remaining in your mind; *the cause of the world*. A world that you can only believe is real. A world in which reality cannot be demonstrated, in any way, or by any means, other than what you think about it.

REALITY

Dictionary definition: *1. A thing that exists in fact, having previously only existed in one's mind. 2. The state of things as they actually exist, as opposed to an idealistic or notional idea of them.*

So what do you think *exists in fact that previously existed only in your mind?*

What do you think is *the state of things that actually exist as opposed to the ideas you hold of them*?

Or better still, don't think about what exists in fact or the state of things that actually exist; instead, demonstrate to yourself their reality.

If their reality exists outside of and has nothing to do with your mind or what you think, then you should be able to demonstrate reality without thought.

Can you? Does reality really exist outside of what you think it is? Can you really do anything other than describe what you think is real?

Therefore, wouldn't reason suggest that what you think is real and what you see as real are the same thing? Just an idea.

The appearance of reality is just that, 'an appearance'. Remember, what you believe the eyes see is just a reflection of light and whatever meaning it has for you is whatever you have given it.

This concept has been repeated in various exercises throughout the book to give you the opportunity to demonstrate to yourself its relevance to the way in which you perceive yourself and the reality of the world around you. It is a concept that is generally met with resistance, as it would infer that 'everything is only what you think it is'.

You may think that it's too simple an explanation and even though you can't demonstrate otherwise you still maintain the belief that it can't be true and that somehow there must be a more complicated explanation to be had. So it is dismissed as nonsense.

The very notion seems to challenge and undermine your whole concept of reality as it does not seem to be your experience and does not concur with what you believe. If it were true then you would have to accept that everything you believe is solely of your making and it is this that you are unwilling to accept. With your current way of thinking it seems incomprehensible so the concept is denied and put out of mind, with little contemplation from a closed minded point of view.

So what do you believe in relation to this concept?

If it is not true, then what is?

How do you demonstrate the reality of anything without thought?

Mind is absolute. Everything you believe and perceive, every action and every reaction, everything you see and feel and hear, the entire universe and everything you experience or ever have, in every minute and in every second of every day, from the moment of your seeming birth to this very moment now, exists only as thoughts in your mind. Whether you think this is true or not is but confirmation that it is, because all you can really do is think one way or the other.

MEMORY

Dictionary definition: *The faculty by which the mind stores and remembers information.*

Your memory is what maintains the illusion of the world. It is where everything you have ever thought and experienced, learnt and seen, heard and believed is held from the moment of your seeming birth to this very moment now. It is what gives stability to the appearance of all physical form, which you experience as something that exists outside of your mind.

In the section on time I asked the question, from what viewpoint do we perceive the present moment?

The answer would be, 'the past'. Without the past, perception has no point of reference to draw from. Without your memories of the past, you wouldn't be able to understand anything in the present. Yet the past is *gone by in time and no longer.* So it must be that what you believe to be your present reality is really just your memory of the past, experienced as the present.

Your memories are referenced by the part of your mind that psychology refers to as 'the subconscious', which is just another name for 'the voice in your head'.

YOUR SUBCONSCIOUS MIND

Dictionary definition: *Of or concerning the part of the mind of which one is not fully aware but which influences one's actions and feelings.*

This is the part of your mind that processes your conscious thoughts. It interprets, analyses, and constructs its own version of everything that you consciously perceive, based on your beliefs, which are established as a result of your constant dialogue with the 'voice'. The subconscious aspect of your mind maintains and directs the illusion of perception by producing the appearance of meaning that is ascribed reality by your past beliefs. It maintains the appearance of all physical action and interacts with your memory in every respect. It is the part of your mind that is responsible for the narration (self-talk) that goes on constantly in every waking moment, questioning and answering itself.

Consciousness (the state of being aware of and responsive to one's surroundings) as it is referred to, seems to be the capacity for the recognition and interpretation of perception. It would seem to enable you to interact with and experience the world, giving it a sense of reality. But what you are perhaps unaware of is that your conscious state is merely a reflection of your subconscious thoughts and beliefs, which are present and operating in every moment and in every instance.

Because you are not generally conscious of your thoughts, it doesn't mean that they are not present in every moment. It would seem as if your memories are thoughts that come and go and once gone they are nothing and nowhere.

But have you ever thought about where they come from and where it is they go?

Your memories remain in your mind. They do not come and go. Every single thought that you have ever had is forever present in your mind.

Remember, in every second of every minute of every day you are thinking. How often are you aware that you are even thinking at all?

Your memories 'seem to be' the result of your conscious thoughts and perceptual experiences from the past and have no influence on your present perceptions. It is believed that they are only impotent thoughts that have no influence or reality of themselves, other than the belief that they can be recalled and thought of consciously in the present. Yet it is in your memory that everything you have ever learnt and experienced, perceived, and believed, remains. And without referring to your memory in every situation and in every moment you wouldn't be able to do or understand anything at all.

So it must be that you are no more conscious of the relationship between your memory and what it is you perceive, than you are of the relationship between your subconscious and your memory. How can you be, since your subconscious is the part of the mind of which one is not fully aware, yet it is your subconscious thoughts that influence one's actions and feelings?

So what you see and believe to be real must logically be the result of what you think and if, for most of the time, you are unaware of your thoughts, then all you must really see and respond to is the result of your subconscious thoughts referenced from your memory and experienced as reality in the present. This produces the illusion of a world that seems to have its own reality, existing autonomously to your thoughts.

For example: you think that you are thirsty and decide to get a drink. You get up from your chair, walk to the refrigerator, open it, select your preference, remove it from the refrigerator, set it down, locate a glass, pick up the glass, set it down, open the drink container, pour the contents in the glass, close the container, open the refrigerator again, put the container back where it was, close the refrigerator door, pick up the glass, take a drink, walk back to your chair, locate somewhere to place the glass, put it down, and then sit back down in your chair.

You have probably done this many times. But can you honestly say that you were conscious of every thought and every action undertaken in order to get your drink? Or did you just simply think 'I'm thirsty' and then get a drink? Other than the initial thought of 'I'm thirsty' and the decision to get a drink, the rest just seems to take care of itself without you having to think about it. But although you weren't conscious of your thoughts, they were still taking place subconsciously, constantly drawing from your memory in every respect and in every moment, directing your every thought and action. Otherwise how would you even know what a drink is, let alone be able to get yourself one?

What if you had to leave your house and go to the shops to get your drink?

How much more could you be unaware of?

Have you ever been driving and at some point realised that for some time you hadn't been conscious of driving at all? Yet you still managed to somehow drive your car and get to where you found yourself. How is this possible?

What about breathing? How often are you conscious of your breathing? Yet you still manage to take a breath every two to three seconds, don't you?

BEYOND CONSCIOUSNESS

Like perception, consciousness is an illusory state; the subtotal of perceptual and conceptual thought. It is the result of dissociation, which maintains your confusion in identity that would see you as a part of the audience, unaware that you are the movie maker.

From my experience there *is* only awareness, which is beyond all illusion and comes from the truth of who we are. Awareness is beyond the ideas of time and space and physical existence. It is beyond perception and consciousness and yet it is forever present, being the expression of what we are right now.

I have used the word 'awareness' in place of consciousness in some of the earlier chapters because it is generally thought of as having the same meaning and so it is more easily understood in the interim. But contrary to popular belief, consciousness as you experience it has no relation to awareness. It is awareness that encompasses your consciousness and because of this it is through consciousness that you will come to recognise awareness.

It is widely accepted by those who study consciousness that it is absolute and represents the subtotal of the unified mind.

Consciousness is categorised into two aspects of mind, suggesting that the mind is split between these two states:

- The finite, being the unified and collective mind, **limited** by perceptual and conceptual thought.
- The infinite, being the **unlimited**, unified, collective mind, devoid of all perceptual and conceptual thought.

Although conceptually it may seem apparent that the mind is split between these two states, mind is whole and undivided. There are no separate states of consciousness—there is only the infinite mind.

FINITE

Dictionary definition: *Limited in size or extent.*

INFINITE

Dictionary definition: *Limitless or endless in space, extent, or size; impossible to measure or calculate.*

CONSCIOUSNESS

Dictionary definition: *The state of being aware of and responsive to one's surroundings.*

This definition of consciousness pertains to the idea of the finite mind in that it alludes to the ability for perceptual experience and conceptual thought. Consciousness does not transcend the idea of the finite mind as it is believed; consciousness *is* the idea of the finite mind. The idea of separate states of consciousness or a 'split mind' is nothing more than the belief that what is whole can be divided.

The appearance of a finite or physical reality is but the expression of the 'free will' of the infinite mind being the unlimited, unmanifest potential for perceptual and conceptual manifestation. In simpler terms, what you choose to believe is what you will perceive. The belief in a physical reality is simply the result of your 'free will' in which you choose to believe it is so.

The infinite mind being devoid of perceptual and conceptual thought is what I would describe as awareness, which by my definition is simply unlimited, unified potential. Being purely potential awareness is only aware that it 'is' and although it is devoid of conscious thought, it is the potential for conscious thought and therefore is encompassing of conscious thought.

Awareness is difficult to describe in worldly terms because the 'truth' just 'is'. Put in worldly terms, you could perhaps think of it like this: Let's use the idea of air to represent awareness.

- In every moment of physical life your existence is maintained by air.
- It encompasses the world and everything in it.
- In every instant you are moving about in it and without it there would be no life.
- The same air is shared equally by everyone. It is not subject to time or place and does not discriminate or withhold its beneficence from anyone.

- You breathe air continually but are rarely conscious of doing so even though it maintains your very existence.

It seems that life still goes on and all of the busy happenings of the world are still taking place regardless of whether or not you recognise your dependence on air. And so it is that the world goes on in your consciousness, having no effect at all on the air, yet it is the air that encompasses your consciousness, which cannot exist without it.

With the air all around you and within you, you cannot but experience its effects even though it is not recognised. All that is necessary to be conscious of it at any time is to simply give it your full attention and there it is, and there you are.

CHOICE

Dictionary definition: *An act of choosing between two or more possibilities.*

So what is there to choose between?

In the world, it would seem that choices are infinite. We exercise the power of choice in every moment of every day. Most choices are concerned with, and centred around the benefit of, the body. We choose what to wear and what to do, what we will eat and where we will go, what we want and what to avoid. These are seen as conscious choices, decided upon in a conscious manner by selecting in order of preference what we deem to be more desirable in relation to what we believe we are capable of choosing between.

At times you believe that you have no choice in what you must do or how you must feel or what has happened to you and feel powerless, as if a victim to circumstances beyond your control.

So, what is it that limits your ability to choose, but your own belief in limitations? For isn't it you who decides what choices you are limited to?

By dissociation you believe that some choices are not up to you and are made for you by something or somebody else apart from your own thoughts and beliefs. At times, you may even feel prisoner to your life, going through the same motions every day, bound by your commitments and responsibilities with no clear end in sight. You become tired and worn and it would seem there is no choice but to serve your time in the hope that someday, somehow your freedom will come. Yet what you fail to realise is that you have been free all along. Your prison never existed and you are only ever prisoner to the belief that your freedom isn't yours to choose.

In truth, there is really no need to choose between anything that can be perceived because all you really choose between are illusions.

Choice is always circular and ends at its beginning. Choice (possible outcomes) = Decision (preferred outcome) = Action (the means to establish your preferred outcome) = The Goal (the result of your choice).

The choices you make are always between what point of reference (+) you will utilise and the goal will always bear witness to the reference you have chosen.

According to the dictionary definition, choice is an act of choosing between two or more possibilities. Only in the idea of time do choices seem to be a necessary function, endless in number and differences, but there are really only two possibilities open to you: the choice is between truth and illusions. In the state of timelessness where nothing did, can, or will ever happen, there is no need for choice because what could there possibly be to choose between?

Yet whilst you still seem to function in the world, if you can accept that there are only these two possibilities to choose from, then your choice is made simple.

- You can choose to see the truth.
- Or choose between illusions.

And what you choose is what you will see.

The way you will see the difference is by releasing your mind from its preoccupation with the past by consistently bringing your mind to the awareness of the present moment. Because now is the only aspect of time that is real and if you would know the truth then you must look only to where it can be found. Everything from the past and all thoughts of the future only exist in your imagination and they are the illusions that you believe to be real.

DECISION

Dictionary definition: *A conclusion or resolution reached after consideration.*

Decisions follow choices and are a call to action. Their purpose is to establish a means or course of action to be taken whereby you believe you can accomplish or bring about the effects of what it is you have chosen.

Like choices, decisions are an attempt to make illusion seem real, in an effort to shape the future as you would have it be.

It may seem that decisions are made consciously, when there is a choice to be made *between two or more possibilities*. But like choices you are also making decisions subconsciously, in every minute of every day.

There can be no action without decision because not only do you decide between your choices but you also decide what course of action to take. You decide what to do and what not to do and exactly how to do it in every moment and for every action. Yet you are probably only aware or conscious of the initial decision and the rest just seems to happen by itself.

Regardless of the choices and the decisions and the actions you take, every aspect will continue to come from your dialogue with the 'voice in your head', until you see clearly that this is so, and consciously choose to withdraw your attention from it. In truth there is really no need to decide between anything because there is nothing to decide. All you really decide between are your choice of illusions, and all your decisions will lead you to, is the illusion of the choice you have made. Yet in the world of perception, your choice is your only freedom, because you have the choice to believe in illusions or the choice to see the truth. What you decide will determine the outcome.

THE THINKER BEFORE THE THOUGHT

This is the true nature of yourself, the 'I AM' that precedes all thought, the place of peace and understanding. It is the place of freedom from all your pain and suffering, the herald of the end of illusion and of healed perception.

It is the conscious acceptance and recognition of awareness, from which you come to reconcile your beliefs.

It is a state of mind that is present and peaceful and still.

It is the condition of an open mind willing to 'just be'.

This is the place from where cause and effect can be distinguished and seen in their proper order.

This is the place from where dissociation becomes recognised and its effects disappear.

This is the place where the unreality of the world is recognised.

This is the place from which you look out on the world and realise that you are its maker.

This is the place from where the ideas of time and space and separation and perception and thought and mind are reconciled.

This is the place where you become aware of the self that is aware.

This is the place where truth abides and all that would hide awareness is brought to reason and transcended.

This is the realm of spirit.

SPIRIT

Dictionary definition: *The non-physical part of a person regarded as their true self and as capable of surviving physical death or separation.*

What is spirit?

The nature of spirit is like the nature of truth, for it is one and the same. It cannot be perceived or described, it just 'is' and can only be known. Therefore, like truth, it is in the undoing or recognition of all that it is not, for it to be known. Spirit is pure potential and it could be said that mind is the expression of spirit.

A common belief is that we are spirits having a physical experience and that spirit existed before physical birth and will continue after physical death. But if the nature of spirit is eternal and physical existence is in time, then there would have to be a pause in timelessness/eternity where time can exist for this physical experience.

At what point in timelessness does time exist?

We are simply spirit, eternal, and the idea of a physical existence is just that; an idea.

There are many views and descriptions of what spirit is; some suggest that individual spirits inhabit individual bodies that have individual personalities and after physical death these individual spirits continue their existence in eternity and inhabit a place called the afterlife.

If you are of religious belief then you may suggest that your physical existence and actions are the determining factor as to whether you spend eternity in a place called Heaven or Hell. And where you go will be decided by a God that will judge your physical actions and determine the fate of your eternal spirit.

Spirit is usually attributed to individuality or separateness and because this idea is accepted in the physical, so is it projected to the eternal. The word 'spirit' is singular by definition, the plural being 'spirits'. It is this same confusion or misinterpretation that leads to the belief in separate truths. Like truth and mind, spirit is singular, it is one.

I have already spoken about my experiences or revelations of spirit earlier on, but for the sake of this topic I will describe this again.

It was as if I was instantaneously encompassed by the most beautiful golden light. All awareness of my body, my surroundings, and even the fact that I was driving was non-existent. Time stopped and as I was encompassed by this light it became all there was and I became a part of the light that seemed to emanate from a presence of which there was a feeling of overwhelming peace and love, like the love for a child, innocent and pure. My appreciation of this love made the feeling more intense and I seemed to sense a warm, welcoming smile, which flowed from the source of this love to my awareness. In a moment of recognition or knowing, it just seemed all so obvious that this was God, the source of my creation, the truth of my identity. This was spirit itself, being the ever expanding love that I shared with all creation, timeless, beyond perception, beyond description.

In these moments of heightened awareness there is a pervasive, unquestionable knowing that I become a part of, a knowledge that seems all so familiar, as if I was simply remembering what I already knew, yet had forgotten.

GOD

Dictionary definition: *(In Christianity and other monotheistic religions) the creator and ruler of the universe and source of all moral authority; the Supreme Being.*

For many, the word 'God' incites immediate defensiveness and is accompanied by thoughts like 'What a load of rubbish, there is no God' or 'I am responsible for my existence, not some God' or 'If there is a God who loves us all so much, why does He allow so much suffering' or 'I am the result of physical evolution, not some divine source that exists apart from me'. In every case, it is the shared belief that there is no ultimate creator or divine source that exists as separate from you, and as you do not perceive otherwise you believe that this is evidence enough that there is no God.

If of religious belief that 'there is most certainly a God', it is generally believed that God is in fact a separate entity that exists apart from and beyond ourselves and can only be experienced through death.

If you look at both cases separately they would appear to be completely opposite ideas. The first suggests that 'there is no God that exists apart from me'. The second would suggest that 'there is most certainly a God that *does* exist apart from me'.

Both ideas can never be reconciled whilst they are seen separately. But from a different perspective, if you take the central themes of both beliefs 'there is a God' and 'there is nothing that exists apart from me', both cases are reconciled as both point to a singular truth. Seen separately, either belief could seem to be true, but this is only because you cannot conceive of a God that is a part of you, whether you believe in God or not.

What God is can only be known and is beyond perception or description, so, metaphorically, I will attempt to draw a comparison based on my experiences.

Let's use the sun as the symbol for God and the light that shines from the sun as the symbol of what we are.

The sun is the source of this light and the light is the effect of the sun. There is no difference between the sun and the light that shines from it and it is like unto itself in every way. Nothing is withheld, there is no boundary or limitation. Its source simply gives all that it is and shines unconditionally and indiscriminately, equally upon all of creation. The sun is the source of life itself and nothing can live apart from its giving. The sun shines constantly as its light reaches to infinity; it is not subject to time, there is no pause in its giving, it is always and forever, complete within itself.

From the world's point of view, it is widely accepted that life is independent of a singular source and that each life is responsible for maintaining its own existence. In this belief, does each life assume the role of creator, as it attempts to prove its individuality and autonomy by creating the illusion of a world of separation in which it can see itself as separate?

Metaphorically, this is like the light assuming the role of the particles, each believing that they are separate and distinct from one another and in this belief forgetting that together, as one, they are the light. Now perception is born. As now it would seem that there is something unlike itself to be perceived. Now must perception take form, as there must be something with which to perceive. And now the ideas of time and space, the world, and the body are conceived in the attempt to demonstrate their separateness. Now the truth is forgotten and the idea of truths is accepted in its place. Cause is attributed to the world and you believe that you are its effect.

Yet the sun has never stopped shining and will always be the cause, and the light has never been separate from its cause, being its effect. There never has been a change in the eternal nature of all that the sun gives and all that is received.

The truth of yourself continues in your relationship with the source, whether you are conscious of it or not. It does not rely on perception or description or even your belief to be what it is. It just 'is', and everything that would seem to obscure it from your awareness is but an illusion of reality, a simple mistake in understanding in the attempt to make real the idea of separation.

God is the source of all life, its expression is love, and you are love's effect, therefore you are love itself. You will come to recognise the truth of yourself reflected in all that you look on with love and you will awaken to heaven in the simple realisation that it was always present and you had never been apart.

If God is love and we are love's effect, why is there so much hate and violence and suffering in the world?

Because the world you perceive has nothing to do with God. The illusion of separation is the result of 'free will', in which the unlimited potential of God is given freely to the mind, which 'wills' to believe it is separate. You are the creator of the world, which only exists as an idea. The material world you believe to be real is a conceptual world, conceived within and maintained in your mind as thought. As it is your interpretation/thoughts that give the world all the meaning that it has for you, then what it is you believe about the world is how it will seem to be for you. What you choose to believe is what you will perceive, and all that you perceive will bear witness to what it is you believe. The only part that God plays in the creation of the world is in giving us the gift of 'free will' through which we are free to express our unlimited potential.

Nothing is withheld by the source of all life. It gives all of itself completely and unconditionally and everything within itself is like unto itself in every aspect. There is no limit or boundary imposed on all that is given, and like our source, we are and have the potential to create the universe as we would have it be. Being purely potential, we are unified within our self, so there is no need for manifestation of any kind because we are everything and everywhere, beyond time and place and the idea of form and separation. Because our source imposes no limits or constraints we have the freedom and power to manifest our desires as we choose.

This is the meaning of 'free will'.

When you use the statement 'I am' in any context you are exercising the power of God over all creation. Being created from God, in the likeness of God, we are everything that God is; therefore the only word that can proceed the statement 'I am' is 'God'.

FREE WILL

Dictionary definition: *The power of acting without the constraint of necessity or fate; the ability to act at one's own discretion.*

Free will is the mechanism by which we create the illusion of a physical world as we would have it be. It gives us the ability to make real, in our mind, the illusion of autonomy and separation and the freedom to assume the role of creator of an illusory self in an illusory world.

Free will dictates the 'laws of attraction' that suggest it is possible to manifest your desires in physical form by way of positive affirmation, visualisation, and assumed realisation. And it is believed that the universe will conspire to make such desires manifest without any consciously directed action.

For example: You 'consciously' desire a luxury car so you consistently imagine yourself owning such a vehicle, as if it is a matter of fact. You visualise yourself driving the car, sitting behind the wheel, feeling the breeze on your face as you speed through the countryside, smelling the leather upholstery, and hearing the engine roar. And so it will come to pass that by some means beyond your comprehension the opportunity will present itself to enable you to realise your desire and own such a vehicle. In short, what you consistently desire will become manifest in your life.

This is also true for all of the bad things that seem to occur in your life, because the laws of attraction do not discriminate between what you deem to be good or bad. The same laws apply to whatever thoughts and images you consistently maintain in your mind.

Although it is believed that the laws of attraction only apply to your conscious thoughts and desires, they are also operating in every moment for every subconscious thought you have. Because you are unaware of your subconscious thoughts it seems as if the situations and circumstances you find yourself in are the result of external influences and conditions and have nothing to do with your present thoughts and feelings. But this is not so. Everything that you perceive is the result of your beliefs and desires, which seem to become manifest in perceptual form through the act of 'intentional observation'.

Whatever you experience in the world is but the result of your own choosing, even though it doesn't appear to be, because most of the time you are not conscious of your thoughts. It is the result of the power of your free will that enables you to **think and believe** whatever it is you like. Free will is the ability to act at one's own discretion. In the world it is thought of as 'freedom of choice'.

It would seem that you are solely responsible for your life and what you make of it. You have the ability to choose what you will do and where you will live, what you want and what to avoid, who will be friend and who will be foe. You decide what is good, what is bad, what judgements to make, and what to believe. You decide how you would like your future to be and what actions to take, what sort of person you would like to be and how you should conduct yourself.

This is the power of your free will, which is present in every moment and from which you create the world as it appears to be. If you maintain the thoughts of hate and violence and suffering then this is the world you 'will' to see and experience. If you 'will' to see love and peace and happiness, then this is the world you will create in your mind. But regardless of what thoughts you maintain and believe to be true, there is no physical manifestation in a physical world; there is only 'unified potential', which is formless by nature.

The world we perceive is conceptual and exists only as thought, the illusion of its reality maintained by the belief that what is perceived is autonomous to the mind (dissociation).

Beyond the illusion of a physical existence, in a physical world, is what we truly will, expressed in our creation from the source of all life. It is simply 'the desire to be as we are', which is the expression of love, extending to infinity, unified and complete within itself for all eternity. This is the real meaning of 'being in heaven'.

HEAVEN

Dictionary definition: *A state of being eternally in the presence of God after death.*

This is an accurate description of heaven, as I have experienced it, except for the idea that you must die in order for it to be realised. It is only the body that would seem to die and the body is just an idea, a confusion in identity as we discovered earlier. It neither lives nor dies as it is only a projection in your mind, a place in the idea of time and space from which you look out and perceive the world through its senses and believe it to be real. The truth is that you are a part of Heaven right now.

Remember, if there is no time then there never was a time that you were anything other than what you are and have always been right now. There is no journey to yourself or to God, for there never was a time that you were separate. There is no journey to Heaven, for there has never been a time that you were absent.

Heaven is not a place. It is the all-encompassing awareness of our relationship with God, the unified source of all potential life. Not life in physical terms but life as the expression of mind in the spirit of love. And when you have brought to reason all that it is not, there it will be, unobscured in plain view, and you will realise that you were never apart, just mistaken. 'God is', therefore you are.

THE WAY TO YOURSELF

Once you have come to terms with the idea that you don't really know who you are, then the road to discovery has begun. Imparted in this material, so far, is another way to think of yourself apart from your body. You are not flesh and bone, you are mind and spirit. And it is to this self that you will come to recognise and understand, through the simple willingness to know. Only when you choose to look beyond the idea of the body for your identity and sense of self can you find yourself.

In this next section we will explore, in more detail, various ways in which you can come to recognise and understand yourself as you continue to bring to reason the validity of your beliefs.

HOW TO ASK AN HONEST QUESTION

The only honest question is one you don't know the answer to.

If you have taken the time to do the exercises and contemplate their meaning, you should have come to the point where it is now possible to understand things from a different perspective. Perhaps you can accept some, but not all, of the ideas presented. Perhaps you've even had your own 'dawning moments of understanding' or maybe by now you are totally confused or unsure of how to put these ideas into practice. Either way, the ideas presented here are accepted and reinforced in your mind by applying them in your life on a daily basis and experiencing their results as you do so. It's not enough just to read the words, you must put them into practice until they become habit. This is all you need do and the rest will take care of itself.

For me it seemed to be a progression of understanding, like pieces of a puzzle that were coming together. As I brought my beliefs to reason the way became clearer, as I recognised that their only truth was that which I had given them.

My reasoning is that if something seems logical yet contradicts what I believe, then the choices are to dismiss it and put it out of mind or to be determined to make sense of it. At times, I was unable to rationalise the logic I found in the ideas I pondered, unable to come to a firm conclusion. It was very frustrating and would usually lead to the thought of giving up, with the reasoning that it was beyond my grasp or intelligence or understanding. But by coming to the realisation that the answers were beyond my range of understanding, I began to ask differently.

The method I use is to take my conscious thoughts out of the equation.

- I think of my question, in simple terms, as I bring my mind to the idea of 'now'.
- I then allow my mind to be still and simply expect an answer.

When my mind is not busy trying to answer itself, it is free to receive the answer. Sometimes it comes as a simple idea, sometimes as if in a dawning moment of understanding, and sometimes as a direct revelation from an awareness beyond time and space. The answers do not come from some divine entity or from somewhere beyond and apart from myself, but from within my mind. The mind holds the truth of ourselves, within an awareness that we all share and in which we exist together, as one with, and as the effect of, our source.

One thought that kept reoccurring to me, during the times when I felt confused or frustrated or unsure of my direction, first came to me after asking the question, "What must I do to progress in my understanding?" I waited in the stillness of my mind for the answer and then I heard a familiar voice say to me, "Just be and you will see." It wasn't a voice that I could physically hear but rather a thought that seemed to communicate this message from within the stillness of my mind. These words have come to my aid on many occasions, reminding me to 'just be in the moment', and when I do so, all becomes clear.

BECOMING CONSCIOUS OF AWARENESS

As discussed before, awareness is the mind that encompasses consciousness, and since consciousness is the medium by which you experience life, it is through consciousness that you will ultimately come to recognise awareness as it 'is'.

Within you is the knowledge of the universe and the power over all creation. All will be reconciled within yourself, as there is nothing that exists apart from you. The good news is that you don't have to look very far to find yourself, because wherever you go, there you are.

To give you a clearer understanding of the goal to which we are working towards, it may help to think of yourself from this perspective: think back to the exercise in 'Your Identity' where we used the idea of a blank sheet of paper to represent the true nature of yourself; pure and clean, timeless and unmarked, the unlimited potential for anything to be written or drawn upon, but in itself complete and in need of nothing to be itself.

The blank sheet of paper represents awareness and the marks you place on the paper represent the illusion of separation, perception, consciousness, and your conceptual sense of self.

Remember, the purpose of this book is not to show you what is 'true' but to help you bring to reason everything that isn't. By doing this you will come to understand that it is you who creates and maintains this false sense of self and the illusions you believe to be true. With this realisation comes your freedom from all of your suffering and worldly concerns as you see quite clearly that their only reality is that which you have given them. As the marks that obscure your 'true self' are erased, the clearer you will see all that you truly are now.

From my experience of being simply awareness, I would describe it to be like 'a unified field of pure potential'. Being solely potential, it is unified and complete within itself. It does not manifest itself in any form because it is beyond all illusion, yet is the potential for all illusion. It is limitless and encompasses the universe within itself. Being eternal, it is timeless and changeless and is always now.

We've discussed at length the concept of time to come to the conclusion that time, like anything else, is simply an idea accepted as the truth and believed to be real. The only aspect of time that has meaning is the present moment now. Now is all there is, now is eternity, timelessness, where nothing ever happened and nothing ever will. Now is the place where you will find yourself when your mind becomes still. It is where you exist and where you are now. So this is where you must come to, in your mind, to recognise yourself.

To practise 'just being in the moment' is simple. You can do this at any time with your eyes open or closed.

First you must allow your mind to be still by withdrawing your thoughts from what's going on in the world around you. This can be done by simply taking a few deep breaths and focusing on the idea that 'there is only now'. Remember that it's not what's happening in the moment, but the moment in which it is happening. If you maintain your focus on this idea whilst consciously breathing, you may find that this is enough to bring you to the present moment.

This is the point you must come to in your mind because it is only from here that all will become apparent. If you find it difficult to still your mind, there are several meditation techniques outlined earlier that will help you to do this.

From this point of present moment consciousness, it is awareness itself that is present in your consciousness. You may not be able to distinguish the difference as yet because, even though your awareness is present in every moment, it is your perception that generally dominates your every conscious thought. And so it would seem that they are the same in experience because you see no contrast between the two.

The clearest contrast is perhaps this:

- Your consciousness is the voice in your head that never shuts up. It is the constant narration and accompanying thoughts that go on and on in every moment of every day.

- Awareness is like the background to your perception. It is the stillness from where your thoughts come (the listener). It is your sense of presence when you allow the moment to 'just be' and the narration has stopped.

So it is that the more you bring your consciousness to present moment awareness, the more this contrast becomes apparent.

Remember, awareness is devoid of all perceptual and conceptual thought, so it is never something that you can label as 'like this' or 'like that'. It can only be known as it 'is', experienced consciously, yet in the absence of conceptual thought. This is what is meant by the term 'just is'.

RECOGNISING ILLUSION– CLEARING THE WAY

The way to undo the illusions that you believe to be real, is by simply recognising them as such. Reason is the mechanism through which you come to see quite clearly that they are not true and by doing so your belief in them is simply withdrawn. They are undone in your mind and will no longer appear in your consciousness, because, as discussed earlier, 'you only ever perceive what it is you believe'. Therefore, when you no longer believe it, you will no longer perceive it.

The following exercise has been presented in various forms throughout the book and is a method of recognising illusion. It is the answer to all of your problems and the cure for all of your emotional pain.

- Take a few deep, conscious breaths and bring your mind to this very moment. Let the idea of time subside with each breath, with the idea that now is all there is.
- Keep your eyes open and quietly observe your surroundings. Don't get caught up thinking about what it is you see, just acknowledge it.
- Now whilst still quietly observing your surroundings, bring to mind a situation that causes you emotional pain. The more hurtful the better. If there is something that you have been carrying around for years or something that often comes back to haunt you, use that. Don't bother to analyse what is more hurtful, just go with your first response and reduce it to a statement like 'because of _____ I feel _____'.
- Now take a few more conscious breaths, eyes open, and bring your mind once again to the idea of now and repeat your statement to yourself.
- Whilst still quietly observing your surroundings, ask yourself the question, "Where is this situation [your statement] that causes me such pain?"

Can you see it in front of you or beside you now? Can you hear it or feel it or sense it anywhere within your immediate surroundings now?

So where is it?

In what manner does it exist now?

It's simply just a memory that you are remembering now. Its seeming cause is past and is *gone by in time and no longer*. It is nothing and nowhere.

So how can you still experience the pain, if its cause no longer exists?

Simply because your present thoughts are of the past and as you bring your thoughts of past cause to the present, you experience its effects (your pain) as if it actually exists now, unaware that this is what you are doing.

Bring all of your problems and emotional pain to reason in this manner. As you do, you are released from past causes and their seemingly present effects will disappear from your mind forever, as you realise that they are nothing and nowhere and that it is you who are responsible for what you think and how you feel.

This is the meaning of 'true forgiveness' which enables you to see clearly that nothing but your own thoughts have produced the illusion of guilt that you would see in other people and that they are as innocent as you are of any wrongdoing that you would hold against them.

Remember, in the present moment, nothing did, could or will ever happen and everything that seems to oppose this rule is but an illusion.

FORGIVE

Dictionary definition: *To stop feeling angry or resentful towards, or to punish (someone) for an offence, flaw or mistake.*

To forgive someone for an offence, flaw, or mistake is judgement, not forgiveness. It is the idea that 'you did this to me and it is because of you I feel this way, but because I am the better person I will forgive you, out of the goodness of my heart'.

This definition would make real the offence and guilt of the other, with no hope of release from its effects, because you have projected the cause of your guilt (your thoughts) onto them, keeping you prisoner to what you think they have done to you. Remember that you are the moviemaker and what you see is just a reflection of your thoughts. You are the one that is writing the script in every moment.

With true forgiveness comes the realisation that the past is *gone by in time and no longer* and because this is so, who can be guilty of anything and deserving of resentment or hate or punishment? Herein lies your freedom from the illusion of past causes and present effects that would otherwise remain as a barrier to your awareness and perpetuate the illusion of dissociation.

When you believe that somebody is guilty of something, it is your interpretation of the situation that sees their guilt. It is your perception that would witness to it and it is in your mind that this occurs.

So what makes somebody guilty then?

Is it not simply just your belief in their guilt that would make them seem guilty?

Although the past is *gone by in time and no longer*, your past judgements still remain in your memory and are believed to be a matter of fact. As you bring these judgements to mind in the present you conceptually relive the event or situation and believe that it must be true because you still feel the effects now.

I met a woman at a Christmas party one year at a friend's house. I hadn't met her before and as we sat and talked, she began to tell me about her recent separation and impending divorce from her husband of around twenty years. She said that he was having an affair with another woman for quite some time before she found out about it. As I continued to listen, I noticed that her smile had gone and I could see the emotions of anger and sadness on her face as she continued her story about how she had been betrayed. She had to leave her beautiful home and now lived in a small apartment. She explained that she was separated from her teenage children, who remained with their father in her beautiful house that was now shared with his lover. She seemed like she was holding back her tears and about to burst, when I said to her, "Have you thought about forgiveness?"

"Yeah right," she said, as her facial expression suddenly turned from sadness to disbelief. "How could you even suggest that he deserves it?"

I said to her, "Think about it this way. It's not about forgiving him, it's about forgiving yourself for what you think about him, and as you forgive yourself for your thoughts, you are released from the effects of how you feel. Isn't everything you just told me related to what you *think* about your situation?"

"Yes."

"And whilst you were telling me what you were thinking, did your emotions go from cheerful to angry to sad and then back to angry and then sad again?"

"Yes."

"Then, can you see that what you were thinking caused you to feel the way you do now?"

"Yes."

"So then forgive yourself for these thoughts and realise that it's not what he did to you that makes you feel this way, it is but your own thoughts that affect you. In this understanding you will see that once you have forgiven yourself, there is nothing left that needs forgiving. You are released forever from the pain you inflict on yourself, when you see it is of your own doing and that it is your choice."

I could see that she was rationalising what I had said to her as our conversation was interrupted by the other guests. Soon after, her smile returned and remained with her for the rest of the day. When I was leaving she came up to me and gave me a big hug and said, "Nobody has ever said anything like that to me before. Thank you so much." I never saw her again but I was sure that she got the message and I wish her well.

With true forgiveness comes the end of illusion, as you simply realise that there is nothing to forgive because nothing has been done.

Dissociation is the illusion that keeps this from being recognised. So if it is to be known then dissociation must be recognised for what it is. I have already covered what dissociation is and presented several examples earlier on, but there are some more subtle aspects that you may not as yet have come to realise.

SUBCONSCIOUS HABITS

Subconscious habits maintain the illusion of time and of separation. They are a way of justifying your belief in guilt, by seeing it in others, with the idea that your innocence can only be proven if somebody else is seen to be more guilty than you. It would seem that the more guilt that you can see in others, the more innocent you become and the better you feel about yourself. This idea, being what you believe, is what you will perceive as you look out on your version of the world.

Being subconscious beliefs, these habits, although continually repeated, are seldom recognised for what they are, resulting in an array of emotions such as fear, anger, hate, frustration, hurt, betrayal, loss, neglect, victimisation, intimidation, superiority, inferiority, and injustice, just to name a few. These emotions then turn towards attack or defence and all of this you would go through to protest your innocence. Yet, you have been innocent all along.

GUILT

Dictionary definition: *1. The fact of having committed a specified or implied offence or crime. 2. A feeling of having committed wrong or failed in an obligation.*

Guilt is the result of listening to the voice in your head, which constantly reminds you of all of the bad things you have done and how guilty you should feel. It tells you how unworthy and lacking and insignificant you are, and through your dialogue with it, provides you with the evidence and all of the reasons why you are. The 'voice' tells you that there will be a price to pay for all the wrong you have done and often reminds you that you should be afraid of the punishment and retribution that's coming to you. And you believe, without question, that what it tells you is true and that this is the sort of person you are.

Because you believe what the 'voice' has told you, you are afraid to look within because you can't bear to see yourself in this light. In an effort to deny how unworthy you believe you are, you attempt to see your guilt elsewhere. So you project your feelings of guilt and fear onto others, in the belief that by seeing them as more guilty your innocence will be proven. This is the way the 'voice' maintains your allegiance and keeps you from questioning what it tells you, and is why you believe its lies.

The projection of your guilt is the purpose of all worldly relationships which provide the means for you to see your guilt externally, in others. Disguised as friendship or love, your relationships maintain the illusion of separation by reinforcing the idea that the guilt that you see is not your own.

Think of a close relationship you have now.

- How often are you guilty of an offence towards the other?
- How often is the other guilty of an offence towards you?
- Which one of you is more often guilty?

What did the 'voice' tell you? Probably something like, "You're the guilty one."

Then you will probably say something back like, "I might be guilty sometimes, but the other is far more guilty than me because …!"

- Think about all of the bad things you have done that you feel guilty about.

You probably don't want to do this because of the way it makes you feel, right?

You may suggest that you have nothing to feel guilty about. But if you're honest with yourself you will see that it is because of how your guilt makes you feel that it is better to be denied and seen elsewhere.

This is why guilt is the foundation of dissociation, creating the appearance of a physical world that would seem to exist apart from your mind, so that you may see your guilt in it in order to protest your innocence.

EXPECTATION

Dictionary definition: *A belief that someone will or should achieve something.*

Expectations are only concerned with future events or situations that you believe should occur. They are consciously derived in your mind through your dialogue with the 'voice'. Based on your subconscious beliefs, they more often become apparent when they are not met and things don't seem to happen as you expected them to, resulting in disappointment or resentment and anger.

You believe the person who has not met your expectations to be guilty of an assault against you and that your anger is justified and their guilt is warranted. But what you fail to realise is that by expecting anything at all of anyone or anything, you simply set yourself up for possible disappointment. It is only you that is responsible for how you feel. All of your thoughts and beliefs about the future are but a series of expectations that will or are likely to happen in time to come. And it is only you that knows what it is you expect. So how can anyone else be held responsible for not being able to read your mind and act accordingly?

Let's clarify this idea a little more with some examples of expectation: you spend your whole weekend morning to night, giving up your only free time to help a friend to move house. What do you expect in return? Nothing?

Two weeks later you ask this same friend if they could help you for just one hour to move some furniture around in your house and they say, "Sorry, I can't help, I'm too busy." How would you feel about this response? What would you expect them to say?

Even though you helped them out of the goodness of your heart or as a favour or even out of obligation for no reward at all, you secretly expect much in return.

- You expect them to appreciate what you have done for them.
- You expect them to make time to help you if requested.
- You expect that there will be no opposition to your request for help in the future.

You may become angry with them or even maintain some sort of lingering resentment towards them. Maybe you will even cease to be friends with them for the injustice of the situation.

What do you expect of your children? How do you expect them to behave?

What about your partner; what do you expect of them?

What about your parents or siblings or friends; what do you expect of them?

How do you feel when they don't do what you expect of them?

Expectations are just ideas. They are thoughts of future scenarios that you imagine could or will exist. You judge their desirability based on your likes or preferences and then decide what action should occur, either by you or by somebody else.

For example: you keep putting off doing something. Why? Perhaps because you expect it to be a chore, unpleasant, difficult, or boring.

This is what you expect and so you judge the task as being undesirable and try to avoid confronting your expectations and getting what you expected. You simply imagine what it will be like and then talk yourself into believing it. Every time you decide to do or not to do anything, it is never the task but always your expectations that you choose between.

So what would happen if you had no expectations whatsoever?

Simply nothing at all would matter and you would be free of all disappointment and emotional upset as a result. It's an easy choice when you look at it from this perspective.

Expectations, being thoughts of the future, perpetuate and maintain your subconscious belief in time and also makes the guilt of others seem justified.

FAULT

Dictionary definition: *A misguided action or habit.*

Do you perceive fault everywhere you look?

Do you see it in people and objects and situations?

The unconscious habit of looking for faults is closely tied to expectation. It is an act of judgement in which you subconsciously search for guilt in other people in order to protest your innocence. Therefore, the more guilty you feel, the more fault you will find in everything around you. The habit of looking for fault is the way that you see to it that your expectations are not met.

For example: when you see other people, do you seem to notice what is wrong with them or what can be improved upon? Are they too fat or is their hair messy or are they wearing too much makeup? Do they walk funnily or are their teeth yellow or their clothes not matching?

Or when you are driving, do you see the car that didn't give way or indicate before a turn or the car that was driving too closely or too fast or too slow?

When someone does something, do you see a better way to do it? Do you see all the mistakes they make? Do you think about correcting them?

In your relationships with others, do you see all their faults? Can you list all of their annoying habits and mannerisms?

How do you expect them to behave?

What role do you expect them to fulfil?

When you look on society, do you see all of the problems and injustices that need correction? And do you fear or hate or despise the things that some people do and believe that they are guilty and deserving of punishment?

By looking for the fault in everything, you cannot escape the effects that such looking will bring. You will experience fear and hate and resentment and hold firmly to the belief in the guilt and punishment that you subconsciously (of or concerning the part of the mind of which one is not fully aware) believe to be your just dessert.

Remember that you will only ever find that which you are looking for and it is **you** who makes the choice.

The way to be free of expectation and the habit of looking for fault is to simply realise that this is what **you** are doing and then make the simple choice not to do so. Be vigilant until it becomes habit and you will no longer see your guilt in the world because you will no longer be looking for it. The world will be transformed before you very eyes and you will come to see your innocence before you.

When somebody asks me if I know what pisses them off the most, I say, "Yeah, you do."

JUDGEMENT

Dictionary definition: *An opinion or conclusion.*

OPINION

Dictionary definition: *A view or judgement formed about something, not necessarily based on fact or knowledge.*

Opinions are your *point of view*, being the subtotal of what it is you believe about something. Like beliefs, opinions are often thought of as fact and make up your view of the world and everything in it. Everybody has an opinion on just about everything. When asked the question, "What do you think?" the answer is always your opinion or conclusion based on what you believe to be true. By having an opinion about anything, you reinforce and maintain the illusion of its reality, not realising that it is but your own conceptual interpretation.

Whatever you judge in terms of what is good or bad, it is always based on your opinion of what you believe to be the good or bad, in yourself, in other people, or in situations that you seem to find yourself in. Judgement, like anything else you are conscious of, is always derived from your subconscious beliefs. Unaware that what you have judged is but a reflection of your thoughts, you don't realise that it is but yourself that you judge because you are not separate from what you think it is that requires judgement. Hence the bible quotation 'Judge ye not for ye shall be judged'.

Only in the idea of time does judgement seem to be a necessary fact of life. Because all of the opinions/beliefs you hold about anything were established in the past, it is with this past reference that you look on the world and believe that your judgements are necessary in order to make sense of it. Yet you remain unaware that it is you who makes the world as you perceive it to be.

All you ever do is but interact with your own thoughts. If something is judged to be good, then it is what you believe to be the bad in you, to which the comparison is made. If something is judged to be bad, then it must be what you believe to be the good in you from which you judge. In the present moment nothing did, can, or will ever happen, and so judgement is not necessary, for there is nothing to judge. Yet while you hold on to the idea of time and space and rely on your perceptions to establish your beliefs, you cannot help but to judge illusions and believe them to be true.

If you would see past all of this nonsense then you must look at it clearly and honestly with an open mind and be willing to listen to reason and you will understand the simple message that 'it isn't so'.

It may seem incomprehensible to suggest that you can live and function in the world without judgement or opinions or expectations, but as you free your mind from these beliefs so you will experience the effects of doing so and as a result you will come to understand that all you ever judge is yourself. With this realisation it is seen clearly that judgement is not necessary and does nothing more than keep you bound to illusions.

It may seem like an impossible task to undo all of these subconscious habits. Firstly, because they are subconscious in nature, secondly, because they appear to be so numerous and seemingly intertwined with each other, and thirdly, because you are perhaps not sure how to.

THE SIMPLE WAY

As complicated as it may seem, I have come to realise the simple way in which these barriers are undone. The key is to remember that these subconscious habits are merely effects and because this is so, once you address the cause, the effects will simply cease to exist. You need do very little to let this be so. All that is necessary is to accept one simple idea and practice using this idea until it becomes habit.

The idea is this:

- Judgement makes illusions seem real in the belief that something has happened.
- True forgiveness is the opposite of judgement and shows you that nothing has.

So if you practice true forgiveness consistently and refrain from making judgements, the effects of your judgements (illusions) will simply cease to exist and you will recognise that your illusions are nothing and nowhere.

The way to practice true forgiveness is in a state of mindfulness: *A mental state achieved by focusing one's awareness on the present moment, refraining from judgement, and allowing the moment to 'just be'.*

UNITY

Dictionary definition: *The state of being united or joined as a whole.*

Unity is the opposite of separation as truth is the opposite of illusion, therefore: Unity = Truth and Separation = Illusion.

The concept of unity is not understood in the world, as it is defined by separation. Unity, by the world's definition, is to accept a specific idea or belief and to give it the status of truth in which it stands by itself, separate from other ideas or beliefs, like being united by country or race or by sexes or religion or in war. It would seem that people who accept and share the same ideas come together in support of a common cause. Yet each one seeks only what they can personally gain from such ideas, which always have an opposite and are unlike each other in every aspect.

For example: to be united by country or race is to be opposed to the unity of another country or race. To be united in a particular religion opposes the truth of another. So it would seem that in the world, unity (*the state of being united or joined as a whole*) has nothing to do with the whole, as it upholds the ideas of separation and difference.

WHOLE

Dictionary definition: *All of, entire, with no part removed.*

Bodies are the symbol of separation, which seem to bear witness to the belief that each body is an individual whole, complete and united within itself. But wholeness is all-inclusive and since bodies never join, wholeness cannot be understood by looking through the eyes of (separation) the body. In the world a united cause is a shared idea that is accepted as meaningful in the minds of those who accept the idea as purposeful and any action that the body seems to take is in response to the cause that the mind has accepted.

So just think for a moment. What do we all have in common and what is it that truly unites us in a common cause?

Perhaps the closest worldly comparison is that together we are one species, united in our humanity on the Earth we all share.

Unity, in the true sense of the definition *(the state of being united or joined as a whole),* is simply the awareness of being united and joined in a singular purpose, being one with all creation. In our unity with the source of life itself there are no separate parts or opposites or differences. Everything shared is received equally and completely. Nobody has more or less, there are no leaders or followers, and nothing exists outside of this unity that is the truth of ourselves.

SEPARATED

Dictionary definition: *Living separately, no longer together, apart, parted.*

As discussed earlier, dissociation is an unrecognised state of mind in which you believe that something can exist autonomously to, or apart from, what you think. This results in the appearance of a world that seems to be the cause of everything that you experience and in which you are merely an effect. With this idea it would seem that you are indeed separate from everything in the world and the illusion of space would seem to prove that you are.

Believing in separation, you think your eyes show you the truth of what you behold and in your judgement you believe that your perception is reliable and sound. You are seldom conscious of the present moment as your thoughts are forever projected to the past or future. Time is believed to be real as separate bodies move about, interact with each other, and then die.

Yet all long we have been forever united with each other in the spirit of love, in the mind that we share, the truth of which we keep from ourselves by believing in a world that would see us separated from each other, confined to and limited by the body's senses. Not realising that together as one is the universe united within us. All worldly beliefs are but an illusion, in a mind asleep, dreaming of separation.

You will come to know yourself when you begin to recognise that you are the dreamer of the dream and that it is only in the idea of unity that the truth can be known, for we are one and that is the truth.

THE SEARCH FOR LOVE

In a world of seemingly infinite differences, what are the common goals that we all share?

The answer is simply: love, and peace, and happiness.

We all want to feel that we are loved and we all want to live in peace and we all want to be happy. We all have our own interpretations of what these things mean and where they can be found, and we all search for them in different ways. But the goals remain the same and it is these goals that we all strive for in every minute of every day. However, they generally seem to be illusive and are only experienced briefly, now and then.

Love turns to hate, peace turns to strife, and happiness turns to misery. Their inconsistent natures lead us to believe that we are unworthy of them or that we are deprived of them by someone or something else beyond our control. We look to the future in the hope that when it comes it may bring with it the love and peace and happiness that we lack in the present. We look to the past for all the reasons why we are undeserving of these things in the attempt to justify why they are not present. And then we continue on in the futile attempt to find what we believe we are undeserving of.

We carry around thoughts like *If only I could find somebody to love* or *If I do this or that or if something else would happen then I could be happy*. Love and peace and happiness are the same thing and they all come together and they all come from the truth in you. They are simply the expression of who you are and are not reliant on future or past or something or somebody else to be.

Think about the first time that you fell in love with somebody.

Were your thoughts consumed with appreciation and acceptance of them? Did you focus on their faults and judge them for all their wrongdoings or did you only look to their innocence? And did you look on this beauty with a burning desire to be forever joined with them in this wonderful feeling called love?

At that time your loving thoughts of them where unconditional and imposed no limit or boundary on all you would give to them and all you would receive from them. In these moments of joining there was only love and peace and happiness. You felt complete and safe and the world around you and all its goings on were meaningless in the light of what you had found in each other and in the joy of what you both shared.

Then in time the light begins to dim, as these all-consuming thoughts of love and appreciation start to become conditional and limited. It would seem that at times the other does not meet your expectations of how your love should be returned. You feel rejected and at times can become bitter and resentful, or even hateful, because of all the sacrifices you have made for them. You attempt to make the other feel guilty for your sacrifices in the hope that if they see all that you have done in the name of your love for them then they will return it to you. The more you expect of them and the more you believe you have sacrificed for them, the more your resentment takes hold, and the more elusive love seems.

Love now seems to be the cause of your pain and although it is all you desire, you believe that it must be avoided at any cost because to love again as you once did would make you vulnerable to the heartache that it brought in the past and would surely bring to you again. Now love has become fearful and to protect yourself you must build barriers to bar its coming or even avoid it completely.

It is seen as conditional and limited and you believe that it can never be what it once was. The barriers are kept in place and continually reinforced and the feelings of loneliness or abandonment and bitterness become all that remains. The meaning of love is lost to you because you have forgotten the conditions in which it came and imposed your limitations and the conditions in which it may come to you.

Recent statistics would suggest that in one in four marriages end in divorce and although there may seem to be many reasons for it, the general response would seem to be 'we are not in love any more'.

So what is love that it can come and go, turn into hate or resentment, and in some cases be avoided altogether?

LOVE

Dictionary definition: *A strong feeling of affection.*

What is love? Have you ever stopped to ask yourself this question? Think now what it means to you.

Do you recall those special moments when you felt love? How did it feel?

Who or what was it that caused you to feel this love? Did you make it happen or did it just seem to come of its own accord?

Bring your thoughts to a particular moment or situation when you felt this love. Can you remember what it felt like? Can you describe it?

The love that you experience in the world is but symbolic, for you still believe that it exists apart from you as something that can be sought and found and as something that comes and goes. To most, love is seen as fearful and painful and is something that can only be expressed to certain people at certain times. To some, love is seen as a sign of weakness and that its expression is demeaning or belittling. To some, love is continually sought after but remains forever elusive. With these beliefs, worldly love is but an illusion, and although true love is sometimes experienced it is but a glimpse of what lays beyond perception and worldly understanding.

Love is **'the expression of spirit in the awareness of the mind of God'**. It is the all-encompassing expression of creation that extends to infinity and is the very essence of your being. It is **'what you are'** and what you share, being forever extended within yourself, at one with God. This definition of love is incomprehensible to those who have not experienced it and to try to convey in worldly terms that it is **'what you are'** is an almost impossible task.

Through NDEs, or near death experiences, many others have described this joining with the source of love and tell of how it was immediately understood to be the very essence of their being. They all agree that nothing on Earth compares to this feeling of love and once joined in this awareness, it becomes all they ever desire.

Love, like truth, 'just is', and it is only what obscures this simple fact that needs to be recognised and forgiven in yourself to see it everywhere and in everything. Love is timeless and changeless, therefore love is forever and always now.

Love is sharing and to give love unconditionally is the way to become aware of unconditional love. Let it be all that you 'will' to see and it will be all that there is to see.

Love waits quietly and patiently in timelessness, awaiting only your acceptance. And when you stop searching for love outside of yourself it will come quietly to rest in peace with you. Just allow it 'to be' and keep no barriers you have made to prevent its coming. For love is the expression of what you are and you have never been absent from yourself.

John Lennon whispered words of wisdom when he said 'let it be'.

WHAT NOW?

All of the ideas and exercises that we have covered so far should have led you to the conclusion that there is indeed more to you than meets the eye. The exercises outlined should have brought more clarity to the understanding of the illusory nature of your beliefs about the reality of the world as you perceive it. Through your meditation/mindfulness practice you should be able to still your mind and see more clearly your thoughts as they arise, as if from an observer's point of view. And above all else, you should be more willing and determined to experience the truth of yourself as you come to the fork in the road, being the choice between truth and illusion. If you have come this far then the road is made easy and the journey's end is in sight as you travel lightly and in peace, only to find yourself at the end of the road.

My experiences of awareness and understanding of consciousness and perception and mind may be contradictory to the current beliefs and teachings of psychology, as are my conclusions of quantum science and its findings. Also, my interpretation of spirit and God may seem to be quite contrary to most religious beliefs. But this is my understanding and worldly translation of the knowledge of the universe in accordance with my experiences as being simply awareness.

The scientific and esoteric concepts I have discussed in this book are derived from a myriad of concepts and sources, so the information provided is compiled from general conclusions rather than individual concepts. As all findings and evidence are conceptual propositions, they are better referenced directly from their source. If you are interested in exploring any of these concepts in greater detail I have found YouTube to be a good platform for information. Useful key terms are 'consciousness', 'the mind', or 'quantum theory' and from here you will find many more related topics.

Once again, the purpose of this book is not to protest what is true but to provide you with a means to see it for yourself. The way forward is clear to me, now, as I received the answer to my final question at the time of writing this book. My question was, "What must I do to bring constancy to my awareness of our unity with God?"

My answer was in the form of a revelation, in which my awareness seemed to expand as an overwhelming feeling of love encompassed my being, as it had once before in the presence of God. An image was projected in my mind of what seemed to be a group of formless representations of people who were a part of a brilliant, golden light and encompassed by the same feeling of overwhelming love. It was simply understood that the answer was to remember that everyone is a part of myself, being the effect of the love of God, united in the wholeness of our source. The way forward is to look only for this in the world, as I think of all others. With this way of looking, the idea of being separate from everybody else would be translated into the awareness of our unity and bring about the recognition that we are one. In doing so, Heaven will be all that remains. It is the lesson of love. So in a mindful state of forgiveness, this remains my practice until I learn this final lesson and all becomes apparent.

With each passing day I experience the certainty of this revelation as I look upon others. A simple smile exchanged in the street becomes a message of love that resonates in my heart and mind. Everything shines with a beauty and an innocence in peace and in a stillness of mind that seems to be all-encompassing. I see in my mind what my eyes do not see, with an understanding beyond my perception. I feel heaven around me and feel safe and secure. I feel loved. I understand that the light that I see around me is but a reflection of myself, as my awareness becomes one with the light.

It is as if I am stirring in my sleep, and in brief moments of waking I see reality as it really is and become aware that I am the dreamer of the dream. Yet I still sleep, but now only lightly. The nightmares have gone now and in peace I dream of Heaven, till we wake in the mind of God.

THE SIMPLE TRUTH

The simple truth, as I have experienced it, is that we are spirit, as one in the eternal, loving mind of God. Within us lies the knowledge of the universe and the power of God over all creation, without limit or boundary. We are changeless and eternal and we are everything and everywhere. We are completely innocent and are as perfect and as loving as God itself. This is our reality beyond consciousness and our awareness of this is heaven.

This is the who, what, and where you are in this very moment now. This is the true nature of yourself.

The purpose of life as we experience it is to simply 'be as we are' and as we are the expression of love it is only through its expression that we will come to recognise our self. The only lesson to learn is that 'this is what we are'. When all we are not has been brought to reason, the 'will' to love will be all that remains and together as one we will awaken in the eternal mind of God.

RECOMMENDED READING AND VIEWING

There are many helpful books and plenty of internet content available if you wish to further explore any of the ideas posed by *The Simple Truth* in more detail.

A Course in Miracles by Dr Helen Schucman
A 365 day course and accompanying text. I have found these teachings to be in direct accord with my out-of-body experiences. It is the way to the truth in you.

The Power of Now by Eckhart Tolle
Provides a good foundation for the understanding and practice of present moment consciousness. Eckhart also covers many other insightful ideas, which can be viewed on YouTube.

The Power of I AM compiled and edited by David Allen
Discusses the power of attraction and free will within the context of 'I Am'. Also available as a ten-part narration uploaded on YouTube by YouAreCreators.

The Headless Way—www.headless.org
Presents practical, simple thought exercises that enable you to contemplate and experience yourself from the perspective of awareness.

International Association of Near Death Studies—www.iands.org
Includes case studies and information related to NDEs. Testimonials also available on YouTube.

www.ingramcontent.com/pod-product-compliance
Lightning Source LLC
Chambersburg PA
CBHW051835090426
42736CB00011B/1816